Taking Control

Enabling People with Learning Difficulties

**Edited by Judith Coupe-O'Kane
and
Beryl Smith**

David Fulton Publishers
London

David Fulton Publishers Ltd
2 Barbon Close, London WC1N 3JX

First published in Great Britain by
David Fulton Publishers 1994

British Library Cataloguing in Publication Data

A catalogue record for this book is available from the British Library

ISBN 1-85346-230-6

Designed by Almac Ltd., London
Typeset by Textype Typesetters, Cambridge
Printed in Great Britain by BPC Books and Journals, Exeter

Taking Control

Contents

Introduction

Judith Coupe-O'Kane and Beryl Smith

This book pays tribute to the many parents and professionals who work and live with people who have learning difficulties. In particular we acknowledge those who respect rights, foster independence and help facilitate means through which those people can, to varying degrees, take control of their actions and lives.

Enabling people with learning difficulties to take control may be achieved in a variety of ways, ranging from systematic application of theory in programmes of learning and development, to a largely intuitive response.

We hope that the issues and reflections raised in this book will inspire all practitioners to continue to adopt an enquiring attitude towards ways in which people with learning difficulties can continue to exert increasing control in the operation and effectiveness of their lives.

Notes on Contributors

MARK BARBER is a teacher at Melland School, Manchester. He has a particular interest in PMLD and is the school's TVE co-ordinator.

JUDITH COUPE-O'KANE is Headteacher of Melland School, Manchester and Education Advisor to the British Institute of Learning Difficulties.

JULIET GOLDBART is a Senior Lecturer in Psychology, Department of Psychology and Speech Pathology at Manchester Metropolitan University.

JOHN HARRIS is Director, British Institute of Learning Difficulties (BILD), Kidderminster, Worcestershire.

HUW JOHN joined Manchester Social Services in 1984 to work with services for people with severe learning difficulties in both Network Management and a development role. He is currently working as Care Manager for Manchester Care Ltd.

ANGELA JONES, mother of Gavin, is the co-author of *Handle With Care*, the true story of her son's early life.

CHRISTOPHER LODGE is a resident of six years standing at the CARE Community in Ironbridge, Shropshire. He has represented his colleagues at the National CARE Conference.

MARY LODGE, mother of Christopher, is a Communication Tutor to adult students with learning difficulties at an Inner City College of Further Education.

ROY McCONKEY is Director of Training and Research, Brothers of Charity, Melrose, Roxburghshire.

SUZIE MITCHELL previously worked as Development Officer in High/Scope UK and is now an Education Psychologist in an Inner London Borough.

STEVE PARKER, previously Headteacher at Fox Hollies School, Birmingham, is Advisor for Special Needs, Schools Division, City of Birmingham.

JILL PORTER is Lecturer in Special Educational Needs at London Institute and has been involved in the training of teachers for severe learning difficulties for a number of years.

BERYL SMITH is a Research Fellow, Centre for Research and Information in Mental Disability, University of Birmingham.

BARBARA SPEAKE is the General Manager of the IHC for the central region of New Zealand.

ALLISON TAYLOR is a teacher at Melland School, Manchester and is the school's curriculum co-ordinator.

CHRIS WILKINSON teaches pupils with profound and multiple learning difficulties at Mayfield School, Handsworth, Birmingham.

KEITH WINUP teaches post 16 pupils with learning difficulties at Mayfield School, Handsworth, Birmingham.

Foreword

Juliet Goldbart

I must confess to having been delighted and flattered to be asked to write a foreword to this timely and interesting book.

Each reader takes from each book a unique experience but, for me, three key themes resonate through the chapters in this volume. First, there is a sense that the views of all authors are deeply rooted in the experience of people with learning difficulties. This enables the reader to move easily from theory and research to their applications, whilst our thinking and our current practice are challenged en route. A second recurring issue is the crucial role of communication skills in enabling individuals to take control of their own lives. The third point concerns the opportunities described by several authors which arise when, within a climate of eclecticism, service providers move away from rigidly behavioural approaches.

In Chapter 1 Beryl Smith provides us with a clear context in the role of research on learning and cognitive development in the education of people with severe and moderate learning difficulties and the extent to which any learning or development thus gained contributes to individuals' ability to exert control over their own lives. She also considers problems of transfer and the role of adults in mediating transfer, thus outlining some general principles which will be exemplified later in the book.

Chapter 2, by Judith Coupe-O'Kane, Jill Porter and Allison Taylor, addresses the implications for curriculum design and implementation and of attempts of teachers to increase pupils' autonomy. Their exploration of these issues leads to the conclusion that teachers must consider meaningful, as well as functional, outcomes of learning. Issues which emerge are those of status asymmetry and hierarchy, of possession and transfer of knowledge and power. Many of these notions fit comfortably with those of radical educators such as Freire (e.g. Freire, 1973).

John Harris's chapter obliges us to look anew at our relationships, both social and communicative, demonstrating the importance of power, influence and negotiation in our everyday interactions. He leads us through to logical compelling conclusions concerning the development of personal power in children with and without developmental disabilities. Whilst without referenced research his lines of argument must remain hypotheses, they are nevertheless plausible, persuasive and exciting.

Chapters 4 (a), 4 (b) and 5 take us straight into the classroom. Chris Wilkinson considers the needs of people with PMLD and how meeting these needs may fit uneasily with a society that values people according to their economic productivity. To counter this, she emphasises the importance of establishing a clear philosophy to underpin the curriculum.

Mark Barber gives us an exciting account of the apparent developmental need to establish contingency awareness. He goes on to describe the potential effectiveness of disrupting the routines thus established in providing a context for the person with PMLD to initiate to attentive others in order to exert control. In doing this he also gives us an unusual degree of insight into the experience of people with PMLD.

The value of establishing predictable routines as a base from which children can deviate recurs in Suzie Mitchell's description of High/Scope (Chapter 5) which presents practical aspects of the scheme in the light of its underlying philosophy. The strategies for transferring control of learning to children will be familiar to those of us in higher education who are working to implement styles of teaching which engender deep approaches to learning (e.g. Gibbs, 1992). Some teachers may feel, however, that Mitchell underestimates how far many schools have moved from a dependency on behavioural approaches to learning.

As if in reply to Mitchell, Richard Byers (Chapter 6) demonstrates precisely how far teachers have come in reflecting on our common behavioural heritage. Echoing Beryl Smith's plea for eclecticism (Chapter 1), Byers suggests that we can retain what is useful in behavioural teaching methods as long as they are balanced by, among others, the more reflective, pupil-led approaches supported by Mitchell. From theoretical issues, Byers leads us gently but firmly to the contemporary theme of cross-curricular planning. Whilst his plea for teaching in context is not new (e.g. Donaldson, 1978; 1978), it is certainly an argument which bears repetition.

In Chapter 7, Steve Parker describes the value of the Technical and Vocational Education Initiative and Records of Achievement in preparing young people with learning difficulties for adulthood and the world of work. He presents a valuable practical example of approaches which raise students' expectations and participation, thus offering opportunities for developing meaningful, functional skills both within and outside the school setting.

Keith Winup (Chapter 8) continues this theme of preparing young people for taking control of their lives as adults in this example of an ecologically valid and highly motivating context for putting into practice skills learned elsewhere in the school curriculum. Readers will find his theoretical support for a School Council, and the preparation required for its effective functioning, valuable.

Barbara Speake and Huw John, in Chapter 9, extend our view of taking control to include helping people to take control of their emotions. They illustrate their twin themes of acquiring skills and ensuring opportunities for using these skills with a description of a self-advocacy event and powerful quotes from its participants. Speake and John support Winup's (Chapter 8) emphasis on the need for training for self-advocacy and committee work.

In Chapter 10, Roy McConkey gives a timely warning that community integration will not of itself result in changes in attitude and transfer of control. He argues that we must take responsibility for changing ourselves and not put the whole burden on people with learning difficulties. McConkey moves us from philosophy to practice, taking tangible and often contentious issues in how the philosophy of increasing control determines the nature of service provision.

Mary and Christopher Lodge and Angela Jones (Chapter 11) provide a salutary reminder that families have often recognised the need for control and autonomy among their members long before professionals. The success of Mary Lodge's model of participatory democracy within the family is evident in her son Christopher's advocacy and self-advocacy skills.

Angela Jones reminds us of the value of a positive and realistic perspective in empowering parents of children with learning difficulties, which, in turn, enables them to empower their children.

Not all of the chapters in this book will excite, interest or even appeal to each reader. They differ, as do readers, in style, philosophy and direct relation to practice. In some books this might be seen as a disadvantage. I would argue that in this volume it is positively advantageous. A diversity of approaches to taking control is likely to influence a diversity of readers and, maybe, open us up to different styles of writing about and thinking about things that matter.

Above all, this book engenders great enthusiasm for a range of good practices; enthusiasm that will be much needed if we are going to meet the challenge of divesting ourselves of the power and privilege of control and passing it over to people with learning difficulties.

Chapter One

Handing over Control to People with Learning Difficulties

Beryl Smith

Handing over control?

What does it mean – handing over control? What is 'control'? There are many definitions, but for the purposes of this book we have chosen a simple one – having an effect on the operation and outcomes of one's life. This interpretation of 'control' does not necessarily mean exercising a full range of choices regarding work, leisure and relationships. This ideal picture of fully determining the operation and outcomes of one's life is an attractive one, but unattainable for the majority of people, in particular those with severe and moderate learning difficulties. Probably the nearest that most of us get to it is by 'having an effect' on the operation and outcomes of our lives. To a greater or lesser degree, we each examine our environments, survey the possibilities open to us in particular situations, take decisions on how to act, we act, and according to the consequences of our actions, revise or consolidate our strategies. In order to have a degree of control over our lives, we need to engage in this 'self-regulatory' process; every step on the way is worth taking, even though we are unlikely to reach the final goal of full control.

Whitman (1990) suggests that it is useful to view mental retardation as a self-regulatory disorder and that because of inability or the lack of opportunity to effectively self-regulate behaviour and the negative consequences associated with failure, people with learning difficulties look to others for assistance. He also points out that lack of self-regulation in people with learning difficulty is not inextricably linked to retardation, but 'rather is a function of a variety of potentially remediable factors such as inappropriate demands by others, over-protective parents, and the absence of experiences that foster decision-making' (p 348).

He cites Shapiro (1981), who attributed dependency and inability to self-regulate behaviour in persons with learning difficulties to the attitudes and practices of 'society'. It may well be that for people for whom the environment is unresponsive or unrewarding, a behavioural state is reached which is akin to that of 'learned helplessness', described in Maier and Seligman (1976). In their experiments, animals which had been consistently prevented from escaping from a painful situation adopted an accepting and depressed stance. Moreover, they did not take the opportunity to escape when this was eventually provided. Feeling that one is ineffectual in exerting control over the environment may well contribute to a state of acceptance and dependency.

For people with learning difficulties there is the added complication that behavioural learning theory, which has had considerable influence on special education, does not recognise the person's contribution to the learning process. While it has been proved possible to teach a variety of behaviours to people with learning difficulties by means of behavioural techniques (Kiernan and Woodford, 1975), it is also difficult to maintain or generalise these behaviours in the absence of external reinforcement. It is difficult for those taught in this way to realise that they need to call upon similar responses in similar situations or produce different responses in different situations (Wood and Shears, 1986). These writers are of the opinion that over reliance on use of behavioural theory in special education does not enable people with learning difficulties to 'make significant decisions about their life circumstances, and directly participate in controlling their own lives'. They attribute this to the teaching of discrete skills which do not have relevance to ability to control one's life and to the way in which skills are taught, because this 'institutionalises independence'.

Whether or not we put the blame for the lack of ability in people with learning difficulties to 'take control' on 'society' or the educational system or some other culprit is not that important. What is important is the identification of procedures for facilitating people with learning difficulties to have an effect on the operation and outcome of their lives. How do we 'hand over control' rather than keeping it in our own hands?

A basic consideration is whether opportunities are made available when the individual has reached a certain age or level of maturity or whether development of self-regulation is a continuous process which should be instituted early in life. If the latter, what are the particular means which are appropriate at succeeding levels of development? If we do not find answers to these questions we may find ourselves in the situation where we are not working to hand over control, but are merely providing arbitrary 'choices' which may or may not be determined by us beforehand. It is easy, for instance, to agree with policy principles invoked when shaping a community service for people with learning difficulties such as: 'Fundamentally, handicapped adults should be involved as far as possible, in decisions which affect their lives' (Punukollu, 1991). This is a laudable intention but must surely be the outcome of a long process of developing ability to make informed decisions about needs, preferences and what one will do and will not do. Exercising choice, being involved in decision making, even at the seemingly simple level of deciding whether to have baked beans or scrambled eggs for supper, for example, requires exercising many mental functions. Drawing on past experience, the relative attraction of the complex of features associated with each dish must be compared, considered, and a decision made. It is possible to opt for one or the other without participating in such a process but, if the aim is to help people with learning difficulties to make informed decisions, from choosing what to have for supper to deciding on what type of accommodation would be best for them, we need to find out how to promote such self-regulatory mental functions.

Fostering development of mental structures and encouraging an individual to direct his own activity with respect to goals characterises education which aims to develop 'interrelationships within a store of information' (Dearden, 1968). Training, on the other hand, aims to develop skills. The following quotation illustrates past attitudes towards people with learning difficulties with respect to their training requirements and their lack of capacity to 'take control'. It also illustrates very well the ease with which those 'in control' can assume that they know best.

> If possible, reading should be taught, for it is a useful accomplishment, but we need not trouble about arithmetic beyond the simplest calculations, nor about writing. As a matter of fact for those who are to spend their lives in institutions, writing may be a source of danger, for they may utilise that accomplishment to send objectionable communications to one another. Games should be organised and under supervision; left to themselves, the feeble-minded have so little initiative and energy that loafing is inevitable. (Potts, 1911, p674)

There have been many and various methods of educating people with learning difficulties since that time, some of which aim to develop self-regulation, some which do not. Fortunately, the opinions voiced above belong to a bygone era but the attitude which permeates the statement may have appeared in another guise in the highly structured, objectives/skills analysis approach based on behavioural theory. (It must be acknowledged that so-called 'behavioural teaching' has tended to remain static despite modifications to the theory.) Wood and Shears (1986) say that acquisition of sets of skills probably provides a 'cloak of competence, afforded by being able

4

to perform certain activities without help'. They point out that producing a 'cloak of competence' by means of teacher control does not encourage participation and interaction on the part of the pupil.

In 1981, McConkey wrote vis-à-vis behavioural teaching '... education is more than activity and ... should be more than "product centred" teaching. Education entails the sharing of knowledge (understanding) so that children come to use it autonomously'. Since that time there has been far greater interest in the educational field in the process of learning as well as in the product. This had led to a more eclectic and interactive approach in which more attention is paid to providing learning situations which are relevant for pupils and which offer opportunities to become involved in their own learning, to take decisions and participate in 'control' of their own actions. The advent of the National Curriculum, which emphasises breadth and balance, relevance and differentiation has further supported a new approach to the curriculum in special schools.

The trend in special education to greater involvement of pupils in the teaching-learning environment is described (Discussion document, NC Development Team (SLD) No 13) as one which encourages pupils to 'exercise choice; participate in decision making; be involved in self-assessment, evaluation and planning; take greater responsibility for their own learning; have greater control over the learning process'. This appears to be a good recipe for encouraging self-regulation as defined above; time will tell if the next generation of people with severe and moderate learning difficulties have benefited. In the meantime it is useful to consider the theories of learning and the associated practice which appear relevant to the aim of 'handing over control' to people with learning difficulties.

Theory and practice of development of self-regulation

During the period in which a behavioural approach to education and training of people with learning difficulties was dominant, many educationalists who felt that it did not recognise the contribution of the individual to his own development turned to theories of child development for inspiration. Piagetian theory was of considerable interest since, rather than conceptualising learning as passive acceptance of input, it emphasises the need for interaction between the organism and the environment in order for mental development to occur (Piaget, 1950). It stimulated an approach to the education of people with learning difficulties which appears to be more conducive to development of self-regulation than does a rigidly behavioural stance. The implications are that by acting on the world the child develops anticipation and understanding of events, termed 'contingency awareness' (Brinker and Lewis, 1982). This represents the beginning of control over the environment with the child eventually making use of increasingly representational means of control in the place of action. Appropriate practice includes provision of motivating experiences or tasks which are matched to developmental level in that they provide challenge but are neither too easy nor too hard. The descriptions of stages in mental development and type of behaviours which are characteristic of these stages facilitates matching of experiences to need.

According to Piagetian theory, adjustment of present ways of interacting with the environment or 'behaving' is said to occur as a result of perceiving that these are inadequate. Increasing ability to 'mentalise' or to manipulate representations of events brings with it increasing ability to plan, review and evaluate one's actions – a dramatic advance on merely 'doing' and one which is a considerable step on the way to exercising greater control.

Most applications of the theory are found in connection with the education of those who are in the sensorimotor period of development (birth to two years in normal development), but are also available for those in the pre-operational and concrete operational periods of development (roughly two to seven years and over seven years in normal development). Stephens was among the first to publish a programme on a developmental /interaction approach for pupils with severe and moderate learning difficulties. The link between theory and practice is described in Stephens (1977). The programme is based on the principle that development proceeds as an individual interacts with objects and people in the surrounding environment. Attention is paid to ecological programming (skill training only when the need for that child is evident), classroom management, classroom grouping and communication programming through interaction with the environment; concerns which are to the fore in educational practice today.

Glenn (1988) has shown that even children with profound learning difficulties, given suitable conditions provided by modern technology, can make choices; in this case between sounds, voices and rhymes provided on speakers. Moreover, they show enjoyment while so occupied and are motivated to further choice-making. At the beginning of this chapter, the opinion was expressed that every step on the way to having more control over our lives is worth taking. In the case of these children, opportunity to exert control, however limited, appears to be leading to increased motivation and increasing self regulation.

The High/Scope programme, described later in this volume, is another example of the way in which Piagetian theory has generated practice which enhances ability to interact more effectively with both the social and material environment. Among its aims is the facilitation of greater self-regulation by giving children the responsibility for planning their own activities and carrying them out independently. 'Planning', 'Doing' and 'Reviewing' are carried out, supported by the adult, using means which are appropriate to the child's developmental level. In this way children become more competent and independent problem-solvers, thus obtaining more control over their environments.

While the original Piagetian theory places considerable emphasis on the importance of interaction with the material world of objects and events and less on social interaction, it is obvious that practice emanating from the theory recognises the importance of the role of the adult or caretaker. It is useful to ask how the child best arrives at the point of beginning to function as an independent agent and what it is about his or her environment that inaugurates such development. Vygotsky (1978) says that the child is assisted to gain competence by 'expert' adults such as main caretakers, competent peers and teachers. These 'experts' provide a structure of assistance which is adjusted to the amount required for the child to succeed on a particular task. By instruction and modelling, adults take responsibility for parts of the task, enabling the child to cope with other components. As the child demonstrates increased competence, adult support is reduced, allowing the child to assume an increasingly independent role. This process appears to be a naturally occurring instructional method used by mothers with their children and is aptly termed 'scaffolding' because it helps children to 'learn how to achieve heights that they cannot scale alone' (Wood, Bruner and Ross, 1976). It can be seen how this approach to teaching is likely to promote the pupil's confidence in his ability to solve the problem, or in other words, to control his environment.

Wertsch (1978), prompted by his links with the Vygotskian school of psychology, is also of the opinion that self-regulation evolves from social interaction, sensitively adjusted to the present level of the child's capacity. He describes an example of adult-child interaction in which the adult leads a child through a problem-solving task; building a tower of toy blocks according to a model. He refers to the various means by which the adult leads the child as 'other regulation'. A person who is able to exercise control in carrying out a task is demonstrating self-regulation, but the young child is only able to carry out certain tasks through other-regulation. In the above problem-solving task the adult regulates the child's activity by providing information about what strategies to use, what comes next, where to look, what to copy and so on. If this is not sufficient to enable the child to carry out the task, the adult may tell the child what to do. Although the adult in this situation is making the control decisions, the child is enabled to complete the task through other-regulation. Wertsch suggests that this assistance, provided by adults at early stages of the child's development, is an important factor in enabling the child to achieve eventual self-regulation.

The concept of shared regulation or other regulation is mirrored in the area of language development (Vygotsky, 1962). Adults first direct children's activities through interpersonal speech and eventually children take over this interpersonal speech to help direct their own activities. This may be thought of as 'shared regulation' followed by 'self-regulation' when the individual is able to use intrapersonal or inner speech which enables more effective control of behaviour.

Shared regulation is only effective as a precursor to self-regulation if the task is slightly too difficult for the child to solve independently. Obviously if the task were far too difficult or already mastered there would be little benefit from such interaction. The reader will recognise here Vygotsky's concept of the 'zone of proximal development' (1981). If the child first acts in conjunction with an adult and then begins to master the strategy which will enable him to self-regulate, the implication for the education and continuing development of people with learning difficulties is that 'scaffolding' to permit choices and decision-making in problem-solving situations should be available from the word go.

Attention to a variety of theories which address early development has inspired many approaches to empowering people with learning difficulties. A report on 'intensive interactional teaching' of pupils with severe and very severe learning difficulties (Watson and Knight, 1991), explains that the changeover from a skills/objectives curriculum was partly due to the feeling that the pupils' day was too predictable and repetitive and that mastery of skills did not always provide pupils with intrinsic satisfaction. Among the results of moving to an interactive approach was that staff implemented a process based curriculum in all areas. They found themselves looking for a lead from pupils, allowing them to manipulate materials, 'building games from pupils' initiations rather than staff's previously decided goals'. The authors are of the opinion that underlying all activities is the recognition of the pupil as an active partner in the engagement – a situation akin to taking part in shared regulation.

Hewitt and Nind (1988), who also emphasise the importance of social interaction, describe the case of a young man with profound learning difficulties whose only means of interacting with his environment was by means of hitting out at other people. Using a model of learning and teaching derived from the interactive processes taking place between mother/caregiver and infant during the first two years of life (see for example Schaffer, 1977; Newson, 1979), they interpreted his behaviour and helped him to interact in more productive and emotionally satisfying ways. He was thus able to exercise a wider range of choice and control than formerly. Hewitt and Nind say that, once engaged in a mutually pleasurable interactional sequence, the individual can safely experiment with further responses and develop new hypotheses.

Another educationalist whose theory and practice is of considerable interest to those who seek to empower people with learning difficulties is Reuven Feuerstein (see Feuerstein *et al.*, 1988). He emphasises the important role played by the chief caretaker in controlling the information received by the child and giving meaning to salient aspects. He considers that such mediated learning experiences enlarge and enrich capacity for intellectual development by developing cognitive functions involved in effective problem solving. If, for various reasons, the child is impaired in cognitive development owing to lack of such mediation, congenital learning difficulties, or both, more frequent and more structured exposure to mediated learning experiences is recommended. This is achieved through use of a cognitive development programme comprising sets of tasks and exercises which goes by the name of 'Instrumental Enrichment'. The exercises are designed to remediate cognitive deficits which hinder or prevent effective problem solving and therefore effective control. Deficits include 'unplanned, impulsive and unsystematic exploratory behaviour', 'blurred and sweeping perception' and 'deficiencies in planning behaviour and hypothesis testing' (Feuerstein *et al.*, 1980). The programme has been used with children and adults with a wide range of learning difficulties. Advocates of the approach are of the opinion that adolescents and adults with moderate and severe learning difficulties can gain a great deal from this approach in terms of cognitive development and attitudes to learning (Burden, 1991). It is often pointed out, however, that the approach is only really effective in terms of increasing effectiveness in overall performance if intensive efforts are made to apply strategies in everyday situations.

A further important contribution to handing over control to people with learning difficulties has been brought about by the examination of cognitive processes by psychologists; ways in which knowledge is acquired and applied in everyday settings. Early attempts made use of a simple computer analogy in which attention is focused on internal events which mediate stimulus-response linkages, rather than on these two directly observable events. The learner is seen as an active participant who selects information, interprets and transforms it, and makes use of it selectively. The theory makes use of concepts such as structural features and control processes. When the model is applied to humans, structural features (comparable to the hardware of a system) are envisaged as a sensory register, short-term memory store and long-term memory store. Information received via the sensory register is either lost or transferred after a very short time to the short-term store. Here, transformation of information takes place before removal to the long-term store from which it can be later retrieved. Control processes (comparable to programmes which regulate information flow through the system) are seen as dependent on subject-initiated strategies.

The model (of which the above is an extremely simplified version) prompted exploration of ways in which control processes could be improved, in the expectation that little could be done about improving damaged hardware or structural features. Strategies to elicit control processes, particularly in the area of memory, were taught to people with learning difficulties in order that they might more effectively plan and monitor their own behaviour.

Researchers such as Butterfield *et al.* (1973) and Borkowski and Cavanagh (1979) generated a host of experimentation, chiefly in the States, concerned with application of these concepts to problem-solving for people with 'mental retardation'. The aim is to improve the adaptive capacity of the person with learning difficulties by developing strategies for approaching new tasks. There is, for instance, a large body of literature on use of memory strategies to aid recall of relevant information and on their effect on performance. Such strategies include rehearsal, grouping or chunking, visual imagery and verbal elaboration (Glidden, 1979). While training people with learning difficulties in laboratory-type situations is effective in improving their performance, there remain problems of transfer and durability as occur in use of behavioural techniques. Accordingly, attention became focused on development of higher level strategies which monitor appropriate use of control strategies.

Even at the time when behavioural techniques were taking a firm hold in special schools in Britain, information was available on use of 'metacognitive processes' (Flavell, 1976, Brown, 1974). According to Flavell (1976) metacognition refers to knowledge about one's own cognitive processes and products and relates to monitoring, regulation and orchestration of these processes when in the service of attainment of a goal. Failure to produce appropriate strategies to solve novel problems, at whatever level, may be due to lack of recognition of the purpose of that strategy. Such goal-orientated behaviour can be divided into a two-stage process. The first, 'planning', includes examining task demands and choosing or developing a strategy for attaining the goal. The second, 'overseeing', involves monitoring and regulating behaviour in accordance with the chosen strategy (Ashman, 1985). Brown (1978) focuses on the role of 'metamemory' in her investigation of ways in which metacognitive skills can facilitate problem-solving. The possible relevance of the role of cognitive processes which control, direct and regulate other cognitive processes to development of people with learning difficulties is exciting and inspiring.

In 1981 Borkowski and Konarski further developed this type of approach by drawing on the Campione-Brown model of intelligence

(1978). This postulates two hierarchical levels of intelligence. One is an 'architectural system' that is involved with processing information; its function being to register information and respond to sensory input. The character of the system varies in terms of capacity (amount of space in short-term memory), durability (rate at which information is lost from memory) and efficiency (characteristics which have to do with selection and storage of information, such as rate of memory search). The other is an 'executive system' whose function is to regulate retrieval of knowledge from long-term memory, enlarge the knowledge base and mediate problem solving.

While drawing attention to ways in which an increase in efficiency at the architectural level might be brought about by improvement of attentional skills and by elimination of inappropriate behaviour that interferes with the learning process, Borkowski and Konarski also consider the relevance of training the executive system. They agree that a learner who possesses sophisticated cognitive strategies and routines 'will likely be an efficient, effective problem solver and display the high-level intellectual skill of inventing new strategies to meet new mental challenges' (Belmont, 1978). This description of an 'efficient effective problem solver' may not match the usual performance of a person with moderate or severe learning difficulties, let alone a person with profound learning difficulties, but is not that the direction in which we would like them to be able to go in order to have an effect on the operation and outcomes of their lives – in short, to take over more control?

Another aspect of the executive system, metacognition, or self-knowledge about cognitive systems and their operation is also explored in relation to education for people with learning difficulties. Borkowski and Konarski (1981) are enthusiastic about the educational implications of the theory for pupils who are 'profoundly mentally retarded' and 'trainable mentally retarded' and even more hopeful about the implications for those who are 'educable mentally retarded'. They support strategy training and training of metacognition as part of the daily curriculum and cite Ross and Ross (1978) whose Primary Curriculum places emphasis on control processes such as following directions, listening, remembering, planning, and problem solving. At least one school in Britain, Staff of Rectory Paddock (1983), attempted to apply such theory in their curriculum for children with severe learning difficulties. They outline a method of developing executive control which monitors the pupil's progress through each stage of the process of developing greater self regulation.

An environment which promotes self regulation?

The theories described above and the resultant examples of practice have much in common, despite the fact that each puts different emphasis on particular aspects. They can help us in our exploration of what goes on when people assume more and more control over their own behaviour and thus achieve an effect on their environment. We can envisage the process of developing self regulation as beginning when the child or adult acts on the environment and develops an understanding of how to control the physical or social world. This is the foundation for further intentional actions which lead to the formation of knowledge structures or schemes which become internalised as development proceeds. These interrelationships between objects, situations and events enable us to make assumptions and predictions which can help us to regulate our behaviour. The better the organisation of these knowledge structures, whether or not they are conceptualised in information processing terms, the more easily and effectively can they be operated.

In their book *Cognitive Strategies for Special Education* (1989) Ashman and Conway advocate the notion of students as active learners and list three characteristics of active learning which are relevant to promotion of eventual self-regulation in people with learning difficulties. They say that (i) learning is not strictly a behavioural or cognitive activity; (ii) learning typically occurs in the company of others; and (iii) 'that we must use existing intellectual skills to deal with the many tasks and learning events that confront us'.

Their first point reminds us that organisational structures or schemes which permit self regulation are only acquired after long periods of learning and experience. Skills which enable the child to obtain information are often acquired and practised in a ready prepared state, rather than 'discovered' by the novice learner. Much knowledge which contributes to organisational structures is the result of routine learning. In this respect behavioural learning is, and always has been, an essential ingredient of the mental development of people with or without learning difficulties. A situation is required in which behavioural and cognitive approaches go hand in hand.

In what way can self-regulatory learning be promoted in people with learning difficulties? In some of the examples given in this chapter the practice associated with a particular theory concentrates on development of separate specific processes involved in taking control. Examples of this are contained in the Instrumental Enrichment approach of Feuerstein and much of the practice associated with an information processing approach. Processes, once developed, are expected to transfer to other situations, or were, until it became obvious that things were not so simple. As with the application of behavioural theory, it is apparent that much effort has to be put into exercising what has been learned in a wide range of situations.

Rather than attempt to teach specific processes in particular situations, lessons from normal child development tell us that these can be better developed in familiar contexts in which the adult provides support but gradually transfers responsibility to the novice. The role of the adult as 'mediator' is emphasised in Vygotskian theory and in Feuerstein's account of mental development. It is not a central theme in Piagetian theory but is important in the High/Scope programme, based on Piagetian theory. Having an adult as mediator in shared regulation situations meets the second and third requirements in Ashman and Conway's description of active learning which promotes self-regulation. Brown and Campione (1986), writing on a 'new look' in assessment and instruction for students with learning difficulties, make a similar point: 'The principles of naturally occurring instructional methods, repeatedly observed as being used by mothers with their children and master crafts people with their apprentices (Greenfield, 1984) can be adapted to successful classroom instruction.' To this may be added the recommendation by Glaser (1984) that cognitive skills be developed in the context of pupils' current knowledge and understanding.

The three characteristics of active learning listed by Ashman and Conway are relevant in the context of this book in which various forms of 'good' practice are described and examined. If we work with children and adults with learning difficulties in situations which are intrinsically motivating and in which they have the opportunity to exercise responsibility for their own actions, the experience of success as a consequence of effort and proper strategy usage leads to increased ability to 'take control' (Whitman, 1990).

Description of 'good' practice' does not seek to decry the essential place that theory and allied programme development plays in the evolution of special education. It draws attention to the reciprocal process by which theory can influence practice and examination of practice can inform and influence theory. In a discussion of the place of the role of psychology in teacher education, Schwieso *et al.* (1992) point out that:

> Only in the relatively recent past have the 'hard' sciences been of direct value to technologists. As understanding within the disciplines developed and confident predictions could be made about the necessary conditions for X to occur, or about the consequences of doing A, B and C, so science came to be of value in practical problem solving and in guiding procedures. Even now there is, in practice, a considerable interaction between theory and application. In addition to its primary problem-solving function, 'applied science' is both a test bed on which the wider validity of theories and data derived from the laboratory can be studied and also a source of knowledge in its own right. *Influence flows in two directions not just one.* (p113, my italics)

Parents and teachers and those who work with children and people with learning difficulties know very well those situations and experiences which promote development and self regulation. Their accounts and reflections are a source of knowledge in its own right and serve to illustrate and illuminate the principles which underlie 'handing over control'.

Chapter Two

Meaningful Content and Contexts for Learning

Judith Coupe-O'Kane, Jill Porter and Allison Taylor

Education is usually viewed in terms of preparation for the future, with the curriculum being formulated within the guiding philosophy of a set of aims. Aims, by their very nature, set out long term prospects. Warnock (1978) refers to the preparations necessary for entering an adult world, the Education Reform Act (DES, 1988) refers to citizenship, an adult phenomenom, and elsewhere there has been an emphasis on independence and the skills required to attain it (Gardner, Murphy and Crawford, 1983). Whilst independence from a professional point of view may constitute a set of skills for the person with a disability, it also refers to being autonomous and able to control one's life (Oliver, 1989; Brisendon, 1986). Personal autonomy has also been seen as one of four main areas that denote the 'coming of age' of adulthood (FEU, 1992), together with aspects related to social interaction, community participation, recreation and leisure, changing roles within the family and productive activity.

By the more farsighted, the development and extension of autonomy has been put forward as one of the main aims of education for pupils with severe learning difficulties (Leeming *et al.*, 1979). Whilst curriculum development tends to stem from ideas of knowledge, skills and understanding it is necessary to examine aspects which relate to what might be termed the hidden curriculum (Kiernan, 1991). This chapter sets out to explore some of the issues and tensions in adopting an aim of autonomy in relation to the role of the teacher, the selection of educational priorities and the development of meaningful contexts for learning.

Being in control

Inherent in the notion of autonomy are aspects related to choice and enjoyment, to decision making and problem solving and to raising self-esteem and confidence. Without these abilities the pupil will be hindered in developing and taking control of his life, even to a limited extent, on entering the adult world. These aspects can be seen to be vitally important not just for determining *what* we teach but for the *way* that we teach. They are also important determinants of the way we interpret the actions of our pupils and our own role. It can quickly be seen that elements of tension exist when we consider our own role and how our *own* behaviour might need to change if we aim for our pupils to develop autonomy.

Implicit in our notions of adulthood is that adults are, and should be, capable of taking responsibility for their own actions and also that they are deemed to 'know better'. There is this implication that adults in general are better able to make judgements than children, have greater foresight and insight into a situation and therefore that their actions are better justified. Expressions such as 'because I say so' did not originate with the child. There is an inherent perceived superiority in the relationship between adult and child. Whilst this may be constantly challenged by mainstream pupils, with a resultant renegotiation of power, it is perhaps less likely to happen in schools for pupils with severe and moderate learning difficulties. In mainstream the catalyst for a change in the relationship may be the pupils themselves and the result is a gradual shifting in the attitudes of adults. The unequal status of adult and child is exacerbated in the special school by two factors. Somewhere along the line pupils have been publicly recognised as having learning difficulties as opposed to the teachers who have not. The concept of 'knowing better' would thus be seen to have official recognition. The second factor concerns the issue of protectiveness. This attitude may translate into a variety of different responses by the adult, not least the desire to protect the individual from the outcome of his learning difficulty. The teacher may be less willing to expose the pupil to risk, to the possibility of 'failing'. Baker (1991) has argued that there is an 'unwitting conspiracy' by both professionals and parents which serves to promote continuing dependence rather than the development of autonomy.

If education is, at least in part, about empowering the pupil to achieve autonomy then the teacher in a sense loses power. In enabling the pupil to take control the teacher is relinquishing control. This creates tensions if our notions of a good teacher include qualities such as being able to manage or control her class, predict and shape the learning outcomes and, through close monitoring and recording, know exactly what has been achieved. The teacher is largely held responsible and accountable for the achievements of pupils. There are additional complex phenomena at work here. Whilst we may be aiming to achieve autonomy we are also aiming to integrate pupils into society. This may be a long term aim which we view as only being achievable post school but at the same time we may feel the need for pupils to go 'unnoticed' in society in the short term. We may feel that for them to draw attention to themselves is to draw attention to their learning difficulty. With this in mind the result may be to work towards a conformity. This is not unlike the early interpretations of normalisation, which was defined by Bank-Mikkelsen (1969) as '. . . letting the mentally retarded obtain an existence as normal as possible'. Such a view was echoed in educational circles (Hughes, 1975) with the emphasis being placed on achieving socially competent and socially acceptable behaviour. It is not surprising that this came to be seen in terms of 'never mind the product, look at the packaging'. It is also not surprising that the very individual nature of the person was lost sight of (Brechin and Swain, 1989) and vastly undervalued. For those working in adult services, one of the concerns has been the nature of the client–professional relationship (Chappell, 1992). For those working in schools this concern has an additional dimension where the relationship is less likely to be one of an equal partnership, or that of a consumer and service provider.

There is a tendency to polarise our ideas of power and taking control: those with and those without; those who do and those who do not. The reality, however, is a shifting balance. With mainstream pupils we have pointed to a negotiation process that is on-going. There is also a tendency to conceptualise it in terms of age – the very mention of adult versus child implies an age marker. Teachers' responses to pupils' initiations may be a function of age. A study by Houghton et al. (1987) examined how teachers responded to children's initiations of preference and revealed that young children were more likely than older age pupils to have their initiations and preferences responded to positively. However, if we reflect on our own lives there are clearly areas in which we feel we have control but also areas in which we feel we have not yet got control. Shifting the balance may therefore be seen as increasing the contexts in which the child takes control; the very nature of play and leisure suggests that the agent has control. Given the need for autonomy to increase it is clear that there should not only be an increase in the types of contexts in which the pupil takes control and the degree to which this is done. The role of the teacher can therefore be seen to be not simply that of imparter of skills and knowledge, but that of a facilitator who devises contexts to which the pupil can bring his existing skills and knowledge and utilise them in a way that achieves an increasing element for which he is in control. It also suggests, however, that some situations must be devised (leading to the development of new skills and knowledge), for which the teacher has more control, for which there is a more predictable outcome, as well as situations in which the learner has control over the outcomes.

Deciding on outcomes

Whilst the outcomes of teaching may be specified in terms of understanding knowledge and skills there is a need to consider the framework in which these will be achieved. For the pupil these are unlikely to be the perceived outcomes, nor necessarily the desired outcomes. At one level we have been encouraged to think in terms of how functional are the skills we are teaching. The measure of 'functionality' is often the extent to which skills are used in the community. An example from the past was to teach the reading of social sight words and the use of money. We can, however, go one stage further and consider the meaningfulness of these outcomes (Meyer, 1991). Whereas the ability to set the alarm clock, for instance, could be seen as a functional skill in that it allows us to get up in the morning at an appropriate time, the usefulness of the skill depends on our motivation to use it. The same criteria can be applied to a whole variety of other independence skills, such as being able to launder our clothes and keep our environment clean and tidy. We can usefully differentiate between actions we carry out for their own sake and actions we carry out because they open up possibilities to achieve other desired outcomes. In determining priorities for teaching we need to ask 'how crucial is this?' and 'how does this build on what the pupil finds enjoyable and relevant?' One of the criteria for selecting priorities must be the extent to which they lead to a meaningful outcome – that is to say, are useful in a range of pertinent situations and provide access to a range of relevant options. The skills, knowledge, and understanding that we select as priorities should be motivating to pupils and the challenge for the teacher is to devise contexts which foster this.

Enjoyment and choice: creating contexts for learning

The utilisation of behavioural principles in teaching has provided us with the confidence that we can enable pupils to achieve new learning. Together with the objectives approach they have, at one level, also fostered a greater sense of clarity of what the learning outcomes will be and consideration of how we can analyse these outcomes into small achievable steps. The past emphasis on providing additional and external forms of motivation may have led to an under-emphasis on what the pupil brings to the learning situation by way of interest and motivation. Kiernan (1991) argues that the 'capacity for enjoyment' is an important goal of education in its own right but one which is given only 'grudging acknowledgement'. Not only can it be seen to be an important goal but also central to devising contexts for learning and acquiring new skills, knowledge and understanding.

Developing the pupil's ability to make choices is an important extension of the capacity for enjoyment. It is a vital achievement on the pathway of achieving autonomy. As Guess *et al.* (1985) state: 'Each choice we make is an expression of our personal autonomy – our freedom to define who we are and what we value'. Being able to make choices is fundamental to feeling in control but these must be real choices (Monty *et al.*, 1979). A real choice occurs where there are two or more attractive alternatives. On the other hand a 'no choice' situation exists where one, or indeed both, of the alternatives are unattractive to the child.

For the pupil to take control, there must be recognition that he may operate a different value system from that of the teacher or of other pupils and that teachers may not be accurate in their predictions of preferences (Parsons and Reid, 1990). Many teachers (in common with parents) will feel uncomfortable with the pupil choosing to do nothing, for example, or engaging in an inappropriate behaviour such as sitting rocking. Teachers may feel that the pupil should demonstrate the full range of his abilities and that the action chosen does not result as a consequence of their teaching. However, if the alternative is unattractive, Monty *et al.* (1979) argue that no choice has been made or indeed offered. What may be the case is that the pupil in doing nothing or engaging in inappropriate behaviour is exercising control in a way that brings some measure of enjoyment. Studies of children with such 'problem behaviour' have stressed the functional nature of that behaviour (Oliver, 1991; Durand and Crimmins, 1991) in that it leads to desired outcomes, or that the behaviour itself is enjoyed by the child. Some recent studies have outlined ways of teaching children to achieve those same desired outcomes in different ways (Carr and Durand, 1985), often utilising choice (Koegal *et al.*, 1987; Dyer, *et al.*, 1990). Another approach has been to teach alternative means to acquire the same, usually sensory, pleasure (Rincover *et al.*, 1977 and 1979). These studies illuminate the way in which the child's interests and pleasures can be used as a building block for the development of new learning. The best of these studies take the function of the behaviour from the child's perspective as a starting point and utilise this knowledge in a way that values this perspective.

If we return to the aspect of choice then we can consider how this provides a context for learning. Interestingly much of the literature is aimed at using choice to increase 'productivity' (e.g. Parsons *et al.*, 1990; Realon *et al.*, 1990). Whilst this may be a questionable outcome there are however some important warnings given. Shevin and Klein (1984) point to the dangers of 'mistaking . . . habitual behaviour for active choice . . . lack of

protest for informed consent . . . and resignation to one's lot for content-
ment with that lot'. Bannerman *et al.* (1990) also warn that 'Inflexible
scheduling often precludes opportunities for choice'. Notions of a well run
school, where a tight timetable laid down by the teacher is strictly adhered
to and pupils have a prescribed set of activities, needs questioning in the
light of opportunities it provides for individuals to develop choice. Choice
is not to be viewed as something that occurs on Friday afternoons or at
milk time. Shevin and Klein (1984) outline five essential aspects of choice
which may be taken as a starting point:

(1) Choices amongst activities.
(2) Whether or not to engage in an activity.
(3) When to terminate an activity.
(4) Alternative means of accomplishing an objective.
(5) Choices of partners for activities.

If we take the stance that no choice exists without attractive alternatives
being presented then it is important to address these points. It may be in the
developmental scheme of things that not only is it an important pre-requi-
site to develop the child's ability to express preferences from a pre-inten-
tional to an intentional level, but that there needs to be a hierarchy introduced in the type of choices presented. If one takes the view that the
hardest decisions are made where the alternatives have almost equal value
then the road to choice making may have to include decisions between
alternatives which are not of equal value. We must not, however, delude
ourselves that the child is fully able to choose until he can operate in equal
value choice situations. One might also infer that the number of alternatives affects the ease with which we make a decision. The immediacy of
the effect of the choice must also be considered together with the amount
of effort required to make it. These are important variables which require
further research and it behoves the teacher to investigate these aspects in
relation to the individual pupil.

We must recognise that such decision making can be a stressful operation. It requires a measure of confidence and self-esteem and these two factors are likely to interact with that of motivation and the relative importance of the outcome for the individual. The level of anxiety may well be
increased if the learner is receiving an unspoken message that there is only
one correct course of action and that the decision making process is about
'guessing' or inferring what the teacher has in mind. As Ainscow and
Tweddle (1988) point out, the anxiety level as a result of the risk taking
may be reduced if the process of decision making is shared.

In placing emphasis on developing the capacity for enjoyment and
choice making skills, there is a danger that this is interpreted in line with

pre-1970 aims where the important aspects of provision were seen by some as limited to 'making them happy' and as freedom of activity (Simpson, 1967). It is not the intention to suggest that teachers abandon planning and all structure. What is required is a better balance between the planning of minute details and overall planning, together with a greater consideration of the experience of education as received by the pupil rather than as intended by the adult. We have put forward the notion of the teacher as facilitator, responsible for creating appropriate contexts for learning, and in so doing creating opportunities for the pupil to take increasing control. This should occur in a growing number of contexts so that wherever possible the pupil reaches adulthood able to make informed decisions and choices which directly affect the quality of his life. In order to promote this, education needs to be viewed as opening up valued options and fostering personal autonomy. It has been suggested that we need to consider the meaningfulness of what we are trying to achieve and the methods by which we are trying to achieve it. One measure of meaningfulness is how crucial the teaching targets are which we set; the extent to which they can be clearly seen to lead to outcomes which are desired by the pupil and which will lead to increasing the options open to him. Choice making has been selected as one particularly crucial skill but it is by no means the only one, nor should it be seen in isolation from the ability to communicate and interact with peers and other people. There are also the important skills of problem solving for which choice making may be viewed as a precursor. However, providing a child with opportunities to develop choice-making skills enables him to express his individuality and demonstrates that we value and respect this individuality.

Meaningful outcomes

Each morning for the past few weeks Paul has been given responsibility for delivering his class register to the school office. At fourteen years of age this young man with profound learning difficulties, non-verbal communication, epilepsy and a limited swallow reflex has just achieved an individual educational priority which was recently set by his teacher. With no support he can now take the register to the appropriate location and return to class.

Natalie is seven years old and has Down's Syndrome. She too has recently achieved and generalised a priority set by her teacher – to obtain a given number of objects up to ten on request. The criterion for success for Natalie was that she would be able to collect, on request, up to ten bottles of milk which are sited in the crates outside the school entrance hall.

The fact that Natalie is learning and generalising the concept of numbers to ten is important in its own right. That Paul can follow through a simple task without support is also an important milestone in his development. Their teachers can tick or record that another skill is achieved and determine a further skill that is deemed as necessary or appropriate.

However, for Paul and Natalie, what might the meaningful outcomes of this learning be? Throughout his school life Paul has been considered delicate and has, at all times, been well supervised and protected for his own safety; he might have a fit, he might go out of school and become lost, he might disrupt other pupils. In achieving this skill of taking the register to the office he has indeed raised the expectations of staff. He does return safely to class, but not immediately. He hands the register to the school secretary or if she is not in the office leaves it on her desk. Having left the register he often chooses to go into either the office of the headteacher or that of the deputy. He passes many people, engaging or not engaging in interaction and negotiates numerous obstacles, such as doors, on his journey to and from his classroom. Each day in this context Paul makes numerous choices and decisions and, furthermore, is eager and obviously motivated to carry out this relatively simple but relevant task.

The meaningful outcomes for Natalie might be equally varied. To collect up to ten bottles of milk involves negotiation of people, doors and PE equipment (if she chooses to go through the hall). Her heavy bucket when returning to the class is a further complication. People interact with her and she with them. In spite of the range of numerous interactions with people and objects she invariably returns with the appropriate number of bottles. For her it may be that the task in hand is incidental. By generalising her skills in a functionally appropriate context, she has opportunity amongst other things to be on her own, choose her own route and engage with others if she wishes.

For these two pupils, their class teachers are professional and diligent in providing a broad, balanced, relevant and differentiated individual programme of learning which ensures continuity and progression. This is achieved through a process of assessment, planning, teaching, recording, evaluating and reporting. Within the framework of the school curriculum the teachers, like any others, have a high degree of autonomy and are responsible for making decisions as to what to teach and how. For their pupils, however, it is important that what is selected to be taught has relevance and is part of a continuum of learning which leads towards autonomy. It is important too that an enriched source of learning is provided which enhances skills, knowledge and understanding. Through the curriculum each pupil should be offered a wide range of purposeful activities and experiences which are considered vital to the development of personality, attitude and overall character.

In many ways Paul and Natalie are typical members of an SLD school community. Their teachers and parents are conversant with most aspects of the Education Reform Act (DES, 1988) and the National Curriculum. Their whole school curriculum now sensitively blends the range of subjects deemed as necessary to teach through extended programmes of study so that a rich and varied range of skills can be identified and taught.

How then can we ensure that what is predetermined by a teacher will be a valuable and relevant learning experience for the individual pupil? Should Paul with his profound learning difficulties be expected to learn skills and experience concepts in geography, history, modern foreign language, religious education etc? Do subjects such as these have relevance when his real priorities are identified as extending his abilities in problem solving, making choices and communicating? His teacher and parents will argue that entitlement to a broad and balanced curriculum is his right. For him the range of curriculum content can be considered appropriate if planning marries the skills which are considered as a priority with those that might not be as essential or accessible but nevertheless valuable to him as a whole person.

RE and a collective act of worship are a mandatory part of the education process; the spiritual, moral, cultural, intellectual and physical development of each pupil being at the core of the educational ethos. When Paul has such obvious intellectual limitations and his needs in early communication and cognition are seen as a priority, is it reasonable to expect him to tackle the varied and sophisticated concepts associated with a subject such as RE? Collective worship for instance tends to be an acknowledged facet of most schools' routine. It is often a whole school event which is sometimes presented tokenistically, and is invariably wedged into the timetable. In such a context Paul might gain little. He may be expected to sit for a lengthy period of time, to supposedly focus on the words or actions of adults and other pupils. However, if addressed sensitively, RE and collective acts of worship can have relevance. Similarly, during daily classroom registration, school assemblies and indeed at any time throughout the day, the development of concepts, knowledge, skills and attitudes for Paul and his peers might be addressed by:

- Promoting equality of opportunity for all class members.
- Promoting choice and responsibility for the day to day running of the environments in which pupils are involved, e.g. planning and organising and taking control of equipment and resources.
- Promoting democracy by encouraging pupils to work as part of a group, developing awareness of others, their feelings etc.
- Enhancing self confidence by giving responsibility and allowing pupils to exert control and make choices.

● Enabling pupils to cope with change; for example, alterations to the daily or weekly routine might be discussed or pupils given opportunity to make and act on an alternative decision.

When teaching subjects and experiences such as RE, collective acts of worship, history etc. it is still important to continue to address the pupils' perceived needs. But generally we, as educators, have a predetermined, somewhat fixed set of notions regarding the content of teaching. This is particularly so in relation to collective acts of worship. Perhaps, for Paul, school assemblies are not the ideal context, although the occasional experience of these might have some meaningful outcomes for him. Aspects of RE can clearly be relevant to Paul and relate to his actual needs. It may be that by organising the context of teaching to suit him the focus of education will place emphasis on a child centred rather than subject centred education.

Cross curricular elements

Teachers of SLD pupils are often considered to be particularly adept and in control of predetermining what to teach, particularly in relation to observable skills. But, by shifting the emphasis away from skill teaching and towards nurturing concepts, knowledge and attitudes, pupils may be in a better position to exert control over their own learning. Perhaps the mysteries of the acknowledged 'hidden curriculum' might be overcome by considering and addressing the cross curricular elements. Through these themes, dimensions and skills it is possible to be more sensitive and prescriptive in promoting and valuing the meaningful outcomes of learning for each pupil.

Cross curricular themes are concerned with the physical, sexual, moral, social and vocational development of pupils. They 'add to knowledge and understanding and they rely on practical activities, decision making and the inter-relationship of the individual and the community' (NCC Curriculum Guidelines, 3, 1990). The five identified themes are Citizenship, Environmental Education, Economic and Industrial Awareness, Health Education and Careers, and these should, ideally, permeate the whole curriculum and learning environment.

Cross curricular dimensions are also valuable in that they promote personal and social education and incorporate equal opportunities and education for life in a multicultural society.

Skills, of course, form the basis of the whole school curriculum and are identified clearly in each subject taught. Cross curricular skills, however, are those which should be fostered across the whole curriculum in a planned and measured way through pupils' individual schemes of work.

Six skills are identified by NCC to be developed throughout the curriculum; these are communication, numeracy, study skills, problem solving, personal and social education and information technology.

Each day Natalie is involved in a range of core and foundation subjects incorporating English, maths, science, RE, horse riding, cookery, integration at a local primary school etc. Her individual scheme of work accounts for all subjects taught, predetermining the many skills she is expected to learn. Through the sensitively developed cross curricular elements curriculum (see annex to this chapter) it is now possible for her teacher also to select those aspects of knowledge, concepts, skills and attitudes which are seen as pertinent to her development.

Citizenship, for example, is about relationships, rights and responsibilities, system structures and forces of change. Through this theme Natalie might be introduced to and gain knowledge of vocabulary; ideas; personal, local, national and global interdependence; rights and responsibilities; belonging; relationships; right and wrong. She might benefit by being introduced to concepts of justice, for example rights (discrimination, responsibilities, injustice), power (control, access, ownership, participation), change (cause, alternatives, development, effect). Skills such as assertiveness, cooperation, negotiation, and problem solving might also be pertinent to her as will attitudes such as empathy, self confidence, self esteem and friendship.

If considered in this way the various subjects and occasions such as collecting the milk, collective acts of worship, English, history etc. can truly relate in a meaningful and functional way to her individual needs.

Meaningful content and contexts for learning

In this chapter, whilst recognising the dilemmas involved, an ethos has been promoted for developing pupils' ability to take control. To achieve a better balance between what and how we teach and the outcomes of this for the pupil it is important to sensitively select knowledge, concepts, skills and attitudes appropriate to the individual and nurture these in appropriate contexts. In this way the outcomes of learning are more likely to be meaningful and will facilitate development towards autonomy.

Annex

Extracts follow (pp31–36) from Melland School (1993) *Cross Curricular Elements: Themes, Skills and Dimensions*. Curriculum Document.

CROSS CURRICULAR THEMES

CITIZENSHIP: Can be seen as political education in its wider sense. This education is the entitlement of all in a democratic society and should be promoted through a whole school approach. Citizenship is about: relationships, rights and responsibilities, system structures and forces of change.

Knowledge	Concepts	Skills	Attitudes
— of specific vocabulary — of systems, structures, ideas — of personal, local, national and global interdependence — about rights and responsibilities — of belonging to, e.g. family, school, social and interest groups — of relationships — of right and wrong	*Justice:* Freedom Rights Discrimination Equality Prejudice Fairness Responsibilities Injustice Inequality, e.g. sexism, racism *Power:* Control Access Ownership Distribution of wealth Language Participation Democracy *Change:* Cause Alternatives Action Development Growth Conflict Peace Effect Stability	Questioning Assertiveness Co-operation Problem solving Planning and Organising Interpersonal skills (e.g. communication) Negotiation Affirmation Conflict resolution Evaluation Thinking critically	Empathy Open mindedness Self confidence Critical awareness Self esteem Willingness to take initiative Caring Friendship

CROSS CURRICULAR THEMES

ENVIRONMENTAL EDUCATION: A new ethic embracing plants and animals as well as people is required for human societies to live in harmony with the natural world on which they depend for survival and well being. The long term task of environmental education is to foster or reinforce attitudes and behaviour compatible with this ethic. To this end, it is vital that teaching and learning about the environment is based on the following perspectives: (a) Local and global, (b) Human and natural, (c) Cultural attitudes, (d) Action for the environment.

Knowledge and Concepts	Skills	Attitudes
— the global environment as well as the local and the link between the two, e.g. climate, plants, animals, buildings etc. — the role of human beings within the environment — the interdependence of human and natural systems — how pupils alone and collectively, now and in the future, can and do influence their local and global environment — that change is an inevitable part of living in the 1990s and beyond — the concept of a sustainable society	— communication with the environment on an aesthetic or spiritual level, be it urban or rural, e.g. art, music, dance — to develop an awareness of the environment by exploring and investigating the physical environment, e.g. educational visits — recognising and analysing different viewpoints and biases — co-operating with others — reasoning and arguing a case — coping with change — participating in action to improve the environment — considering value judgements about what is better	— a concern for the well being of the earth and its inhabitants — a desire to protect and improve the environment — recognition of the need for humanity to live in harmony with the natural world — a belief that it is possible for people, working individually or with others, to make an impact on how the world develops and changes — a positive outlook for the future rather than a doom laden pessimism

CROSS CURRICULAR THEMES

ECONOMIC AND INDUSTRIAL AWARENESS: Is concerned with helping pupils at all stages in their lives to make sense of the world in which they live and to participate fully in society as far as they are able or have the desire to do so.
D.E.S. the curriculum 5-16 curriculum matters No.2, HMSO. 1985.

Knowledge and Understanding	Skills	Attitudes
— of key economic concepts — of business enterprise, e.g. 'butty' business — of industry and work, e.g. work experience — of consumer affairs, e.g. shopping — of technological developments — of Govenment, Economy and Society — of working roles within the immediate and extended environment, e.g. mum, dad, teacher, policeman etc.	— to collect, analyse and interpret economic and industrial data — think carefully about different ways of solving economic problems and making economic decisions — distinguish between statements of facts and value in economic situations — comminucate economic ideas accurately and clearly — establish working relationships with adults outside school — co-operate as part of a team in enterprise activities — lead and take the initative — handle differences of economic interest and opinion in a group — communicate effectively and listen to the views of others on economic and industrial issues — to experience different community locations, e.g. shopping centre, garden centre etc.	— an interest in economic and industrial affairs — respect for evidence and rational argument in economic contexts — concern for use of scarce resources — a sense of responsibility for the consequences of their own economic actions, as individuals and members of groups — respect for alternative economic viewpoints and a willingness to reflect critically on their own economic views and values — sensitivity to the effects of economic choices on the environment, e.g. recycling — concern for human rights, as these are affected by economic decisions

CROSS CURRICULAR THEMES

HEALTH EDUCATION: Should support and promote attitudes, practices and understanding conducive to good health.

Knowledge	Skills	Attitudes
— of substance use and misuse, e.g. drugs, smoking — of sex education — of family life education — of safety of the individual — of health related exercise — of nutrition, e.g. healthy eating: choices at lunchtime — of personal hygiene — of environmental health — of psychological health — of appropriate behaviour	*Caring:* for self, others and the environment. — develop personal hygiene routines — employ safe working practices — recognise/prevent hazards — basic first aid *Coping:* making and dealing with relationships — assertiveness and conflict resolution — change, physical, emotional, social, living techniques — developing survival strategies — maximising quality of life *Choosing:* working with others. — finding and using information and services — analysing, assessing and evaluating — decision making/alternatives *Communicating:* discussing our thoughts, ideas, feelings — sharing — listening	— self respect, self esteem and self confidence. — commitment to care and improvement of own and other people's health, the health of the community and environment — awareness of other people's needs, emotions and feelings — willingness to explore values, beliefs and practices of different cultures and groups — responsible and critical attitude towards the effects of individual and economic decisions on health — concern for the rights to health care, concern for justice, democracy and equality, positive attitude towards equal opportunities

CROSS CURRICULAR THEMES

CAREERS: The provision of careers education and guidance should help pupils through their education to develop skills, attitudes and abilities which enable pupils where appropriate to be effective in a variety of adult occupations and roles. Careers education should help pupils to: (a) know themselves better, (b) be aware of opportunities, (c) make choices using information, (d) move smoothly to new situations. These aims should help to promote five strands in pupil's development:

Self	Roles	Work	Career	Transition
Pupils begin to form impressions about themselves: — increasing self-awareness and forming ideas about personal preferences — understanding that pupil's knowledge of self, roles, work and career is influenced by their own viewpoints — further development of personal and social skills (e.g. self assessment, negotiation, assertiveness etc.)	— developing ideas about roles at work — extending understanding about the variety of work roles and their inter-relationships — understanding that perceptions of work roles will have both similarities and differences to those held by other people — developing ideas about roles within the family, e.g. brother, sister, etc. — developing ideas about roles within the community, e.g. milkman, fireman etc.	— developing and describing ideas about work — exploring various types of work, identifying feelings people associate with work, carrying out simple classifications of categories of work — understanding that work opportunities in different locations will vary, and that work can be a controversial issue	— understanding that personal interests and abilities provide a basis for thinking about choices — understanding the implications of present actions for their own future career possibilities	— beginning to appreciate the nature of change — preparing pupils for changes brought about by moving to a new school/class — understanding that change is an integral part of life — preparing pupils for the transition from school to continuing education, training or employment

CROSS CURRICULAR DIMENSIONS

Cross-curricular dimensions should permeate the whole curriculum.

AIMS: Cross-curricular dimensions promote personal and social development through the curriculum as a whole. NCC documentation identifies dimensions as including equal opportunities and education for life in a multi-cultural society. Manchester LEA supports the aim of a curriculum which meets the needs of all regardless of physical, sensory, intellectual, emotional or behavioural differences, gender, sexual orientation, socio-economic, cultural or linguistic background, religious, racial or ethnic origins, so that:

RATIONALE: Pupils see their own and others' origins, differences and contributions in a positive light.

● The curriculum will be relevant and accessible to all pupils, will validate and extend their experiences and relationships
● Self esteem and mutual respect will be generated
● Pupils are equipped to make informed choices and decisions
● Pupils are able to participate in the decision making processes recognising the opportunities and limitations involved

Dimensions to consider when preparing a pupil's Individual Scheme of Work:

Personal	Habitual	Spatial	Temporal	Media
e.g. Gender Race Age Disability Ability Equality Responsibilities etc	e.g. Home environment School environment Work environment Play environment Social environment Holiday environment etc	e.g. Immediate environment Local environment Regional environment National environment European environment Global environment etc	How people are affected by or can affect change e.g. Today Yesterday Tomorrow Next week Next year etc	e.g. Direct personal experience Experience of friends/family Comics/magazines TV Radio etc

Chapter Three

Language, Communication and Personal Power: A Developmental Perspective

John Harris

> In a culture like ours, long accustomed to splitting and dividing all things as a means of control, it is sometimes a bit of a shock to be reminded that, in operational and practical fact, the medium is the message. (Marshall McLuhan *Understanding Media*, 1964)

The power of mass communication in modern society is self evident. The television has become pre-eminent as a vehicle for transmitting news, information and entertainment and few people see a day pass without spending some time watching broadcast programmes. It is hardly surprising that politicians, at least the successful ones, have become adept at using television to achieve their own ends nor that, in countries in which the transfer of political power is achieved through violent means, control of the radio and television services is seen as an essential prerequisite of a successful revolution.

On a smaller scale, interpersonal communication is also habitually harnessed to the exercise of power. Indeed, part of what we mean by linguistic competence is the ability to use language to influence other people (Hymes, 1971). Children acquire this kind of political skill in the use of language and communication by serving an apprenticeship with competent and therefore relatively powerful practitioners. Moreover, in order to facilitate the learning process, the expert practitioners must not only share power with the child but must also deliberately create situations in which the child has the opportunity to influence other people. To see how this is achieved, it is necessary to explore, in some detail, the relationship between personal power, communication and language during early child development. This will provide a basis for a consideration of difficulties which may arise when a child is unable to use language and communication to exercise interpersonal power. A number of recommendations are made regarding the role of adults in working with children who, because of developmental disabilities, experience problems in learning language and other means of communication.

Personal power

Part of what we mean by 'being a person' is that we have the ability to exercise personal powers (Shotter, 1973). Personal powers concern, first of all, our ability to organise our own actions in ways which enable us to achieve particular outcomes. For example, if I am thirsty and want to drink from the cup in front of me, I can deliberately initiate actions which will result in the liquid in the cup being transferred to my mouth. This development of this ability to understand the relationship between desired outcomes and the means to achieve them has been described in great detail by Piaget and Inhelder (1969).

Personal powers also enable us to participate in a social world. Here personal power is expressed to the extent that we are able to influence other people in order to achieve specific outcomes. For example, we may wish to request assistance from another person. This might involve a request for information (Do you know whether this machine takes pound coins?) or action (Would you pass me the menu?).

The exercise of personal powers in relation to the physical or material environment requires an understanding of outcomes associated with different bodily actions. For example, reaching, grasping, holding, dropping, throwing, carrying, kicking, blowing, walking, running, climbing, sucking, etc., all have more or less predictable outcomes, depending upon the objects or materials towards which the actions are directed. The development of this kind of understanding usually occurs within the first two years of life and, following Piaget, is often referred to as sensory-motor development.

In contrast, the exercise of personal powers in the social sphere requires an understanding of how other people are likely to repond to particular actions. Whereas the outcome of actions on objects can be reliably predicted from the action itself and characteristics of the object to which it is applied, one person's response to the actions of another will be determined by how that action is *understood and interpreted*. Interpretation of other people's actions is determined by a host of factors, including the context or situation and our relationship with that person. Consider the simple action of raising one arm. For a pupil in a classroom, this is likely to be interpreted as a *request* for attention from a teacher; it conveys the pupil's recognition of his own inferior status and the power of the teacher to decide when the child will be given an opportunity to speak. The same action, performed by an adult in a restaurant, is likely to be interpreted as a *summons* to a waiter of inferior status who is expected to comply immediately.

The capacity to interpret similar actions as having different meanings rests upon our ability to recognise actions as expressions of intention; a teacher must recognise that a pupil who raises his hand is requiring permission while a waiter must see a customer's raised hand as a summons. Moreover, the pupil and the restaurant customer must believe that their actions will indeed be interpreted in this way; their ability to exercise personal power in particular social settings is determined by their understanding of the meaning of their actions for other people. 'I know, that he knows, that when I raise my hand I expect him to respond immediately.'

Power and language

Language can play an important mediating role in the exercise of personal power. For example, language may be used to help monitor and control actions and ensure that they are co-ordinated and directed to a particular end (Luria, 1959). A simple example involves the covert rehearsal of instructions which guide us in the performance of a complex task, such as preparing egg soufflé or finding a new address in a strange town; the actions required for producing the soufflé or arriving at our destination are coded in language; success is assured if we can organise our actions to conform with these instructions. Of course, this, in itself, is a complex skill which requires monitoring of external events in relation to the sequence of instructions. 'After the second set of lights turn right' or 'Cook until light brown'. If we are not confident that we can remember the instructions we might well write them down.

Language is also a powerful instrument for influencing other people. As a consequence, our ability to influence others and to assert our own personal powers is to a great extent determined by our linguistic abilities. Extending power through language requires abilities which extend beyond a command of vocabulary and syntax – so called grammatical competence (Hymes, 1971). Just as the use of actions to achieve social ends requires an understanding of how actions are interpreted, so the use of language to influence other people requires knowledge of the way in which people respond to what we say in different settings. There are many similarities in

34

the way in which we exercise power through actions and through speech. This is underlined by the use of the term *speech act* to describe the relationship between what people say and what they seek to achieve through language (Searle, 1969).

In order to use language as an instrument of personal power, it is necessary for the speaker to make predictions about the way in which a listener will respond to what he or she says. The effective speaker is able to adjust what is said, and the way in which it is said, to meet the needs of the listener and to achieve intended outcomes. This involves adopting the listener's perspective – putting yourself in the other person's shoes – and making predictions about how he or she is likely to react. For example, when confronted by a child who is upset because he has lost his favourite toy, we might want him to stop crying. While the command 'stop crying' would neatly express out wishes, our appreciation of what it feels like to lose something we value might suggest a response which is more sympathetic and more effective.

Speech acts

An analysis of spoken language in terms of speech acts reveals a number of elements or actions which together determine the impact of language on other people.

(1) The **utterance act** is the physical production of sounds which can be recognised as words and sentences. (For example, it's ten o'clock and the train leaves at ten thirty.)
(2) The **propositional act** involves using words and sentences to describe the world around us. (As I speak, the time is ten hours after midnight and I know that a particular train leaves the local station in half an hour.)
(3) The **illocutionary act** is the effect which words and their meanings are intended to have on other people. (The person I am speaking to is irritating beyond belief! I want her to travel to the station now in order to catch the train.)
(4) The **periocutionary act** is the actual effect of words and sentences on other people. (My house guest collects her bags and leaves.)

From this perspective, effective communication is about making other people understand what our intentions are. We may want the other person to tell us something, or to act in a particular way; we may want them to know something; we may even want to elicit a particular emotional response from the other person. Influencing people by speaking to them can be relatively straightforward, for example, when I ask the greengrocer 'How much are your apples?' or when I say to one of my children 'Turn the television off and come and eat your tea'. These examples illustrate direct speech acts in which the content of what is said directly expresses the outcomes which the speaker wishes to achieve. On other occasions, the relationship which exists between speaker and listener or other aspects of the social setting prohibit the use of such direct speech acts. In such cases, we frequently turn to indirect speech acts, such as the example given above. On occasion, people will go to extraordinary lengths to achieve a particular outcome by using indirect speech acts. Consider the following conversation between two people on a train (Byatt, 1990)

> 'We are travelling together' he said. 'We decided – you decided – to come. What I do not know is whether you would wish – whether you would choose – to lodge and manage yourself separately from me after this point – or whether – or whether – you would wish to travel as my wife. It is a large step – it is attended with all sorts of inconvenience, hazard and – embarrassment. I have rooms reserved in Scarborough where a wife could well – find space. Or I could reserve other rooms under a false name. Or you may not wish to take this step at all – you may wish to lodge separately and respectably elsewhere. Forgive this baldness, I am truly trying to discover your wishes. We left in so exalted a state – I wish decisions could arise naturally – but you see how it is.'
> 'I want to be with you' she said.

From this example of speech being used by adults to advance an intimate and complex relationship, we turn to the question of how children are introduced to the power of language and communication.

The development of personal powers

> Human beings have no personal powers at birth at all; they only gain them in negotiated interaction with those who already possess them (Shotter, 1973, p154)

Human infants are given little choice but to become part of a social world. From the moment of birth they are, to varying degrees, kissed, cuddled and comforted, fed, bathed, dressed and undressed according to the customs of those around them. Above all, they are treated as social beings. Gradually, their biological systems which control cycles of sleep and wakefulness, hunger, feeding and defecation, are synchronised to conform with the social routines of those who care for them. This is achieved, in most cases, with remarkable speed and relatively little difficulty.

As part of this process, infants are inevitably presented with frequent opportunities to engage in simple repetitive interactions with caregivers. Moreover, as they grow older, there are increasing intervals of time which are not devoted to satisfying biological needs. Within a matter of weeks, infants demonstrate not only a fascination for other people, but an ability to recognise familiar faces, voices and smells. They are also beginning to phase, or 'mesh', their behaviour with the actions of their carers (Schaffer, 1971; 1977). For example, simple repetitive actions such as hand waving or vocalisations will be co-ordinated with the actions of caregivers. Of course, this does not happen by chance or indeed without the connivance of adults. On the contrary, adults are extremely adept at responding to the behaviour of infants in such a way that they make simple interactions possible.

At this point there is no suggestion that infants *understand* what they are doing; more importantly, they are not acting *deliberately* in order to achieve a particular outcome. It is true that an infant can exert extraordinary power over his caregivers, for example, by crying when hungry or hurt. However, it is important to distinguish these natural powers, which exist solely by virtue of complex biological systems, and the exercise of personal power which is marked by deliberation and intentions (Shotter, 1973).

The gradual emergence of personal powers is only possible because adults, who are vastly more powerful than infants, are prepared to create simple interactions in which the behaviour of infants has social consequences. This is accomplished by the adult acting *as if* the infant's behaviour were intended to achieve a particular outcome, even though this is clearly not the case. For example, the language and behaviour of mothers and fathers suggests that they regularly interpret natural 'events' such as burping, defecating, and hand waving as if they were deliberate acts with social significance. It is only by being exposed to the social impact of non-deliberate actions that infants become aware of the potential for exercising personal powers. For example, it is difficult to resist the temptation to respond to a very young baby who waves his hand, even if we doubt that he shares our appreciation of the social significance of hand waving. By the age of six months, infants understand that they can usually elicit some kind of social reaction by hand waving and most adults will oblige by 'waving' back. A little later they will understand more specifically what waving 'means' and in what circumstances it can create a particular social effect.

As infants become increasingly able to play a social role and to engage in social interactions with adults, so their ability to exercise personal powers increases. To the extent that they are able to express their intentions so that other people become aware of what they wish to achieve, they succeed in communicating illocutionary acts; to the extent that other people are instrumental in fulfilling those intentions, they succeed in performing periocutionary acts.

The emergence of first words provides an alternative medium for communication and the exercise of personal powers. Typically, first words are used to convey a limited number of direct speech acts and, in many respects, they mirror the communication acts previously expressed non-verbally. They include:

- **Labelling** For example, saying 'baby' while holding a toy doll.
- **Repeating** For example, saying 'dinner' after hearing an adult say 'dinner'.
- **Answering** For example, when an adult points to a picture and the child answers 'car'.
- **Requesting action** For example, unable to fasten a button the child holds it up and says 'do it' to an adult. (Dore, 1974)

A little later, children aged about three employ a wider range of speech acts. However, they are still relatively simple insofar as the meaning of the words is directly related to desired outcomes.

- **Requests** For example, 'What's that?'
- **Descriptions** For example 'I'm making a big house' (while playing with Lego).
- **Statements** For example, 'That's right, it goes there'. (Dore, 1977)

There is some way to go before children become adept at using indirect speech acts to achieve social objectives, for example, using a comment 'Gosh, I'm hungry!' as a device for obtaining something to eat. Much of what they have to learn is not specifically about language; rather, they have to learn the social conventions in their community governing such things as status, probity and politeness. They also have to learn that when it is inappropriate to exercise personal powers through direct speech acts, it is often possible to achieve similar outcomes indirectly. For example, it may be more acceptable to say 'I promised my mother I'd be there for tea' rather than 'I'm bored with your company and I want to go home'. Finally, they must master the productive use of direct and indirect speech acts to match an infinite variety of social situations. Their success in using language to influence other people will depend upon the acquisition of additional grammatical competence but, more importantly, it will require a considerable increase in social sophistication.

Power over things and power shared with other people

> Every function in the child's cultural development appears twice: first, on the social level and, later, on the individual level; first between people (interpsychological) and then inside the child (intrapsychological). This applies equally to voluntary attention, to logical memory and to the formation of concepts. All higher functions orginate as actual relations between human individuals. (Vygotsky, 1978)

Personal powers are expressed in two ways; by actions which result in predictable outcomes on inanimate objects and by actions which are intended to produce specific effects on other people. There is considerable disagreement regarding the way in which personal powers in these separate domains are related during development. Piaget argued that, given opportunities for infants to explore the world of objects and inanimate things, biological structures are preadapted to respond by creating mental structures which enable the infant to represent means–ends relations; the development of personal powers over objects occurs independently of the infant's experience of social interactions.

An alternative view, and one which will be considered in rather more detail here, is that it is only through participation in social interactions that the child becomes able to acquire any personal powers at all; personal powers are first acquired as a result of interactions with caregivers and are only subsequently extended to the performance of deliberate actions on objects. How is this social explanation of conceptual development and the emergence of personal powers justified?

When a child directs his actions to attain specific ends, he must know what he is doing and why; he must have purpose in mind; in other words, he must be able to *represent* not only the world as it is now but the world as it might be as a result of his actions. For an explanation of the emergence of representation, we turn not to the evolutionary and developmental adaptation of biological structures favoured by Piaget but to a closer examination of the child's experience of the social world.

At birth, it may reasonably be supposed that infants have no ability to differentiate various categories of experience; they are certainly well equipped with the sensory apparatus needed to detect and distinguish sensory experiences (for example, see Bremner, 1988), but they provide us with little evidence that they can understand and make sense of what they see and hear. An important first step in this process is the awareness of 'self' as an entity, bounded by the physical limits of a containing body, and separate from the external world which is revealed through sensory impressions.

As the infant is enmeshed, willy nilly, in interactions with caregivers, he is, as we have said, treated as if he were already social; by treating his actions *as if* they had social significance, caregivers highlight the connection between actions performed and their social consequences. Caregiver responses provide the infant with an opportunity to see his actions reflected in systems of social meaning. From making spontaneous movements which are guided by sensory impressions such as hunger, pain and discomfort, the infant gradually begins to act *in order* to elicit social reponses. In making this transition, he must view his own actions as elements within the web of meaning created by his caregivers. The subjective 'self' of direct experience is gradually complemented with the 'self as others see me' (Mead, 1934).

Exposure to social experiences leads the infant on, first to a form of participation where his actions are incorporated and interpreted by others with or without consent. Because other people interact on the assumption that the infant is able to act intentionally and to exercise personal power, he does *in fact* exercise power although, initially, without deliberation or intention. Action in order to achieve particular outcomes, that is, with deliberation and forethought, requires that the child considers the relationship between his own actions and those of other people; he must not only 'feel' his actions as a subjective experience, but must also come to 'see' his actions as others see them. Intentional behaviour in the social sphere involves the ability to represent actions and their significance for other people before they are executed.

A further consequence of being able to consider one's own actions as others see them is the ability to understand actions as means to possible ends. With the emergence of representation in a social setting, the infant also becomes able to separate the world as it is, from what it might become as a consequence of transformations brought about by his own action. Indeed, it is through joint interaction around objects such as balls, rattles, cups and food items, that a child is gradually introduced to an ever increasing range of possibilities for action sequences which impose order and structure on the physical world. These might include placing one object on, or inside, another, grouping objects together, banging one object against another, and making patterns or shapes with objects. Such action sequences, first practised in co-ordination with an adult, are subsequently extended and developed, as they are applied to an ever increasing range of objects and materials. Powers which are created through social interaction are personalised and, subsequently, used in both social and solitary activities; they are used to negotiate and communicate with other people and to order and control the physical world.

The role of adults in the child's acquisition of personal powers

During development adults play an important role in both helping the child to acquire personal powers and in teaching the child how to exercise personal powers in ways which are socially acceptable. This includes the following:

(1) **Creating the conditions whereby the actions can be treated as socially significant** For example, adults typically establish simple games or social routines with infants. The game format creates a framework of shared understanding within which actions can be seen as having meaning. (Bruner and Sherwood, 1976)

(2) **Responding to the actions as if there are expressions of intention**
As we have already seen, infants only become aware of the social significance of their actions because of the way in which adult interpretations are reflected back to them. Consider Vygotsky's account of the
relationship between a child's attempt to grasp something which is just
out of reach and the point gesture:

> Initially, this gesture (pointing) is nothing more than an unsuccessful attempt to
> grasp something, a movement aimed at a certain object . . . When the mother
> comes to the child's aid and realises his movement indicates something, the sit-
> uation changes fundamentally. Pointing becomes a gesture for others. The
> child's unsuccessful attempt engenders a reaction not from the object he seeks
> but *from another person* . . . the primary meaning of that unsuccessful grasping
> movement is determined by others . . . later, when the child can link his unsuc-
> cessful grasping movement to the objective situation as a whole . . . The grasp-
> ing movement changes to the act of pointing. (Vygotsky, 1978, p 56).

(3) **Helping the child to conceptualise alternative outcomes** For example, by offering choices – a child is offered a choice between a drink of
juice and a drink of milk; or by re-running interactional sequences with
slightly different outcomes – the game of 'round and round the garden'
is changed so that the child is tickled under his arms, across his tummy
or under his feet.

(4) **Showing the child that other people have personal powers** To some
extent awareness of other people as social beings with interests,
desires and the capacity for intentional action goes hand in glove with
the development of personal powers. What is often more difficult for
young children to accept is that their own powers are limited and can
only be exercised with the indulgence of adults. The power of verbal
and non-verbal communication is determined by the responsivity of
the participants.

(5) **Helping the child to compromise and negotiate** This might mean
changing objectives or desired outcomes or choosing among different
means which are available to achieve a specific outcome. For example,
a child who requests an ice lolly, but is offered a biscuit, can either
accept the alternative outcome of the request or devise another action
(such as crying!) which might be more effective. More sophisticated
strategies involve delaying gratification (I can't have it now, but
maybe I'll be more successful later when she's finished watching
Neighbours) and taking turns (You can have a go; then it's my turn).

Personal powers and developmental disability

The apparent ease with which children are assimilated into a social world
is misleading; as we have seen, the process is complex and of immense

developmental significance. Furthermore, the integration of adult and infant patterns of interaction is finely tuned and, therefore, susceptible to disruption from a variety of individual and situational factors. Observational studies have shown that a variety of developmental disorders including Down's Syndrome, autism and sensory deficits make the establishment of complex interactional patterns which usually occur between parent and infant highly problematic. Parents and carers are likely to feel confused and frustrated and, as a result, may be reluctant to provide opportunities for social play. Young children with disabilities are, therefore, at risk of additional disadvantages because they are deprived of the experiences which seem to be necessary for the development of pre-verbal communication. Furthermore, the more serious the child's disability the greater the degree of disadvantage is likely to be; those with profound and multiple disabilities are particularly vulnerable. If unable to 'connect' with adults and actively participate in the world of social experience, instead of developing personal powers, children with learning disabilities are likely to become increasingly vulnerable and powerless.

The acquisition of language is also invariably affected in children with developmental disabilities; this is partly because the primary impairment affects the representational and cognitive abilities necessary for language and partly because these children are often deprived of appropriate experiences. However, it is important to remember that language is part of a developmental process which begins with adult–child interaction and the appearance of pre-verbal communication. Children who fail to master communication at a pre-verbal level are likely to have difficulty in communicating with language: the linguistic skills they do acquire may stand out as being awkward and used in socially inappropriate ways. In such children, mastery of linguistic form is separated from the emergence of personal powers and, as a result, it is diminished as an instrument for communication.

Developmental implications

If, as a result of any one of a number of primary disabilities, an infant fails to acquire personal powers, the developmental implications are far reaching. To complicate the picture further, children and young people with severe developmental disabilities are always at risk of being treated in ways which reduce their opportunities to exercise personal power. Throughout childhood and adolescence, they face a struggle to influence other people and through this to take control of their own lives.

This can be made clearer by looking at difficulties experienced by children with different developmental disabilities. To begin with, consider the child with multi-sensory impairments. As babies, such children may be particularly difficult to 'reach' and may seem uninterested in the usual patterns of interpersonal play. Because they have impaired vision and hearing, they are likely to find it difficult to 'tune in' to interactions which rely upon seeing the other person's gestures and facial expressions or hearing words and other vocalisations. Their own actions and expressions are also often difficult for adults to interpret; the social significance of their actions may seem unclear or inconsistent. It is not, perhaps, surprising that, very often, attempts to establish communicative interactions end in frustration and confusion.

Infants and young children with sensory impairments frequently engage in stereotyped behaviour patterns, such as rocking, eye poking and patting or stroking objects against their bodies. Rather than an instrument for social exploration, action becomes a source of cyclical self-stimulation. Other people are excluded and there is no opportunity for the child's movements to be incorporated with the actions of a sympathetic adult; the usual mechanism for making sense of infant actions within a sequence of interactions is missing. While adults may want to understand the meaning of the child's actions, they are shut out and denied the usual clues to interpretation. The action remains solitary and essentially meaningless.

More serious from the child's point of view is that the first stage in acquiring personal powers, the distinction between the 'subjective self' of inner experience and the 'self as others see me', is undermined; sequences of self-directed actions create a closed loop within which the subjective 'I' is stimulated and self awareness is denied. The child's actions may be considered deliberate in the sense that a particular action is associated with a certain sensation, but there is no social support for the exploration of alternatives and the explication of choice. Even more significant is that, without the opportunity to participate in a world where actions are understood in terms of their meaning for others, the stimulus for the representation of experience is absent; the environmental 'push' to deal with the world in thoughts, as well as actions, is missing.

Some children seem to acquire an understanding of their own powers in relation to the world of objects but appear totally confused by social interactions with other people; attempts to influence other people tend to be mechanical, almost as if they expect people to respond in the same predictable way as objects. More importantly, they seem unable to use actions to infer what other people want, or hope to achieve. This inability to make sense of other people in terms of the mental states which guide behaviour is most noticeable among children who have been diagnosed as autistic. Some researchers have suggested that it is the primary deficit for these children and that other 'typically autistic' behaviours and disabilities are a direct result of their poorly developed theory of mind (Astington and Gopnik, 1991).

From the perspective presented in this chapter, autistic children illustrate a number of important points. First, they show how much we rely on making sense of behaviour in terms of its social meaning and how difficult interacting with others becomes if this ability is impaired. Very often autistic children have difficulty in making sense of simple gestures such as pointing, beckoning and waving goodbye and they may not understand the significance of facial expressions; because they cannot work out what other people might *want* from a situation or how other people might be *motivated* to act in particular ways, they often seem naïve or insensitive.

Secondly, because of these difficulties, autistic children find it difficult to influence other people; some autistic adolescents may not have developed the range and variety of interactional styles usually associated with pre-verbal toddlers. Non-verbal communication is problematic and their attempts to exercise power over others often seem crass and socially inappropriate.

Thirdly, without the foundation skills for using actions to communicate, their acquisition of language is impaired. While some autistic children do acquire spoken language, even to the extent of using quite long and grammatically complex sentences, their ability to use language to influence others is invariably much more limited. Their command of speech acts is usually restricted to direct acts where the meaning does not have to be filtered through the medium of social knowledge and expectations. One example of this is the tendency of many autistic children to ask direct and very personal questions on meeting someone for the first time.

A relatively large number of children with severe learning difficulties are not autistic, but nevertheless demonstrate a range of inappropriate behaviours; these include, among other things, destruction of property, aggression towards others and sometimes self injury. Other less serious but nevertheless disconcerting behaviours, such as a refusal to co-operate with others and deliberate non-compliance at crucial points in an activity, for example when boarding a public bus, are also common.

When children with developmental disabilities present behaviours which are difficult to understand in terms of what we know about social interaction and communication, teachers and parents are often uncertain how to respond. They may decide that all attempts to engage the child in social interactions are pointless and simply stop trying. Rather than being treated as a person who has the potential to communicate, the child's communicative difficulties gradually become accepted as part of his or her pattern of disabilities. Another reaction is to over compensate for the child's limitations by doing things to him and for him, but without providing appropriate openings for the child to respond. Adult–child interaction is gradually replaced by adult *directed* action in which the child's role is to conform and comply. A third reaction is to emphasise the repertoire of socially meaningful actions which are currently displayed to the exclusion of opportunities for establishing other more elaborate interactive sequences. All of these responses are limited because they fail to recognise communication as a dynamic process by which children gradually come to exercise personal powers.

Children who find communication difficult and unrewarding may gradually opt out of social activities altogether. The concern here is not with those children for whom 'opting out' is an expression of choice, for example, when they wish to avoid certain tasks or activities, but with those who gradually spend more and more time on their own or on the periphery of social groups because they do not understand how to participate in even simple social routines.

While maintaining their isolation, they may explore a wide range of different behaviours and the effects which these have on their surroundings. While it is easy to ignore behaviours which don't make sense (in that they are not part of a recognised pattern of actions and interactions), given sufficient time, most children will, sooner or later, present a behaviour which other people regard as offensive or dangerous. At this point, the response by surrounding adults is likely to be dramatic. To the extent that the child's action produced a noticeable reaction from other people, it becomes endowed with considerable social significance. For children with few resources for influencing the behaviour of other people, inappropriate behaviours can become potent instruments for exercising personal powers.

Such behaviours do not need to be executed in a planned or deliberate way. Provided the behaviour is sufficiently inappropriate or dangerous or disruptive, it is likely to elicit a noticeable reaction from nearby adults and, as a consequence, it will gradually attain social significance. To the extent that the child enjoys the resultant attention, or is bored by the activities which are temporarily disrupted, or prefers the social isolation which is imposed as a 'punishment', the behaviour may inadvertently have produced a wholly desirable outcome.

From a developmental perspective, this might be regarded as a huge leap in terms of the child using actions to influence other people. Unfortunately, the emergence of 'challenging behaviours' is beset with additional complications. First, adults, rather than seeing the behaviour as developmentally progressive, are likely to see it as 'a problem' which needs to be dealt with. Adults are likely to be more concerned with eradicating the behaviour rather than incorporating it into a meaningful sequence of interactions. Even the gentle teaching strategies proposed by McGee and his colleagues

(McGee *et al.*, 1987) represent a deliberate attempt to replace inappropriate behaviours with more appropriate forms of social interaction and communication.

Consistent adult responses, for example ignoring the child's action, are likely to confirm or reinforce the link between that action and specific outcomes, such as being left alone and not having to participate in social or educational activities. On the other hand, inconsistent responses which are, nevertheless, predictable and dramatic may also help to establish the action as a powerful tool for manipulating adults; with time the child may even begin to use the behaviour deliberately to achieve a range of different outcomes depending upon a variety of situational cues. Paradoxically, in this situation, the child is being provided with enhanced opportunities to acquire the complex communicative skills which may, hitherto, have been unavailable.

The second complication is that behaviours which are perceived as 'problems' seldom become the focus for play and the elaboration of social routines. While the child may acquire very considerable power to influence others through the presentation of a 'problem' behaviour, there is very little opportunity to extend this into interactional sequences which, in other circumstances, would help the child to explore and refine the meanings which can be attached to simple actions. In contrast, adults are usually caught in the contradictory position of wishing to reduce the occurrence of a problem behaviour and feeling that they must respond when the behaviour reaches a particular frequency or level of severity. The inevitable outcome is that the child learns that the way to ensure the behaviour produces an effect is to perform it more frequently or more intensely.

Exercising personal powers in schools

Development during childhood usually involves a progressive change from a position of relative impotence to one in which the individual is able deliberately to influence his or her surroundings, including other people. Younger children and those with developmental disabilities are inevitably less powerful compared to older, more able, children. The task of parents and teachers is to provide social and educational opportunities which enable children to acquire personal powers and to exercise those powers in ways which are considered socially and culturally appropriate. While this process seems to happen remarkably easily under ordinary circumstances, it is often disrupted when parents or teachers encounter children with severe disabilities.

Schools are complex organisations which rely upon rules and expectations in order to function; explicit rules and implicit expectations determine the power relations between adults and children. For example, in my daughter's school, one of the rules states that 'pupils will obey instructions from teachers immediately and without question'. Similarly, teaching is usually interpreted as taking place within a relationship where one person tells, shows, or helps another person to do something; the student or pupil learns, to the extent that he or she complies. Resistance, dispute or refusal is not compatible with instruction. Thus, for most children, success in school is achieved because they submit to the power of adults. Of course, this does not mean that children are unable to exercise power in their relationships with adults, only that they choose not to.

For children with severe developmental disabilities, the situation is rather different. Very often they are very compliant because they have no other options; they are still learning what it means to exercise personal powers.

Ordinary schools operate on the assumption that children already have a clear understanding of the different power relations which may exist between adults and children, how these vary in relation to the social context and the behaviour which is deemed appropriate in different situations. By conforming to adult expectations, children demonstrate their knowledge of social relations and their competence in managing their personal power. In contrast, schools which serve pupils with a developmental disability have a responsibility to facilitate and encourage the development of personal powers. How can this be achieved?

To begin with it is helpful to consider the practices which are unlikely to promote the development of personal powers. At the beginning of this chapter, it was suggested that infants first recognise their own potential powers because adults respond to their actions *as if* they were already deliberate attempts to achieve particular outcomes. Conversely, any assumption that the actions of a child with a developmental disability *do not* have a communicative function, removes the possibility of responding in a way which illustrates a social meaning. In this way, the expectation that a child is unable to use actions in a socially meaningful way easily becomes a self-fulfilling prophecy.

In a similar way, the assumption that pupils are unable to make choices, or that choice is an impractical luxury which must give way to organisational and curricular priorities, will lead to fewer opportunities for learning about personal powers. How many pupils with profound and multiple disabilities are regularly asked if they wish to use the toilet or to be changed – and more importantly, how willing are adults to interpret small movements, facial expression and vocalisations as ways of saying 'yes' and 'no'? Assisting others to acquire personal powers requires that we voluntarily relinquish some of our own powers; this can be inconvenient, especially when it means that the achievement of some of our own objectives (having everyone ready for lunch by 12.00 p.m.; getting the art materials ready for the next lesson; working towards National Curriculum Attainment Targets) must be delayed or temporarily suspended. Since most of our social experiences are shared with others who exercise their own personal powers within mutually agreed limits, sharing power with children or young people whose behaviour is sometimes confusing and unpredictable also requires considerable personal confidence and some courage.

Formal instruction can also reduce the opportunities available for exercising personal powers. Good classroom control is widely regarded as a *sine qua non* for effective teaching; but control can mean many things. Providing materials and a structure designed to encourage thinking and learning is one way of achieving control. Another way involves providing a narrow range of options and coaching the child until he or she demonstrates a particular sequence of behavours. Behavioural teaching techniques are typical examples of instructional procedures which are effective precisely because they operate to maximise the adult's influence over the behaviour of the child. This may be effective in establishing particular skills, but success is bought by reducing the range of permissible social interactions.

In spite of organisational constraints and conventional wisdom about the role of a teacher, schools abound with opportunities for enhancing pupils' awareness of their own personal powers. Social interactions occur throughout the school day, in a variety of settings and as part of many different activities. In many instances, it only requires awareness and a slight change of emphasis on the part of the teacher to make communication a central feature of a practical task or a teaching activity. Adults can help pre-verbal children to create new meanings from actions and interactions. For those who are beginning to use words and phrases there are opportunities to find out how words can be used to influence people in different ways (for example, consider the word 'me' used in response to a question – who wants a drink? – and as a way of attracting attention) and to learn new words to replace actions (for example, naming items as a way of requesting instead of using reaching or pointing).

In order to help children to acquire personal powers, it is necessary to create situations where adult power can be relinquished and shared. When adults interact with babies and infants this happens spontaneously. In the case of pupils with disabilities and particularly when children attend school, it is more difficult. Nevertheless, the implications of this developmental perspective are clear. By denying children opportunities to experience actions as expressions of social meaning, we limit their understanding of what it means to be a person; the role of social experience in establishing individual abilities is diminished and the capacity to use actions and words to communicate with other people is placed in jeopardy. Language and communication are too often treated as subjects to be taught or skills to be learned. Instead, we should think of them as the medium by which we exercise our personal powers and negotiate to achieve intended outcomes – in operational and practical fact, the medium is the message.

[**Author's acknowledgements** Some of the ideas expressed in this chapter were first developed during conversations with Margaret Cook, Heather Murdoch and Dawn Wimpory. I am also grateful to Dave Hewett and Heather Murdoch for their detailed and constructive comments on an earlier draft. I should like to thank Grace Simmonds for her meticulous typing of the manuscript.]

Chapter Four

Profound and Multiple Learning Difficulties

(a) Contingency Awareness: Putting Research into the Classroom

Mark Barber

Contingency awareness occurs when a person attempts to create an event or spectacle with the understanding that his or her actions are linked to external (or internal) results. Piaget (1952) described the first appearance of contingency responding in his son aged around 10–14 weeks. He observed that Laurent deliberately moved his arm in an attempt to hit a mobile that was attached to his cot. This, he considered, indicated movement from the stage of 'primary circular motions', during which infants do not appear to link their own actions with outside events, to the stage of 'secondary circular reactions' at which children show some anticipation and understanding of results. Subsequent workers have generally confirmed that contingency responding is demonstrable by three months of age (Millar, 1972; Lewis *et al.*, 1985), although Watson (1966) reported that it could be detected earlier when observing behaviours already fully established in the infant's repertoire. Awareness of co-occurrences or contingencies is considered to be the foundation on which all subsequent learning develops and also represents the beginning of means of control over the environment.

However, for individuals with profound mental disabilities and additional or associated impairments in motor functioning, ability to engage the physical environment is considerably reduced. They may cease responding when their responses do not produce repeatable consequences, leading to what Brinker and Lewis (1982) term 'secondary motivational handicaps'. When working with students who have profound learning disabilities, it is important to (a) understand the processes by which mental development proceeds, and (b) circumvent the barriers to further mental development, as far as possible.

Background literature on early cognitive development

Although there have been challenges, modifications and extensions to the theory of early development of cognition proposed by Jean Piaget, his description of development in the sensori-motor stages (0–24 months in normal development) has generally been confirmed. Indeed Glenn (1986) considers that:

> . . . in the study of intellectual development there is no question that the most influential theorist in the last 50 years has been Jean Piaget.

There are two main premises of his theory which have particular implications for consideration of development of contingency awareness in pupils with profound learning disabilities. The first is that development is the result of complex interactions between the child and his/her environment, and this has been generally substantiated by other writers, for example Vygotsky (1978), Brinker and Lewis (1982). The second premise is that the general sequence of development is both universal and invariant. Although it has been demonstrated that the early cognitive development of profoundly and multiply disabled children proceeds in much the same way as in other children, there have been relatively few studies in this area (Woodward, 1959; Khan, 1976; Rogers, 1977; MacPherson and Butterworth, 1981), and some disagreement as to the precision of the parallel developments, but it is generally acknowledged that developmental frameworks are applicable for people with profound and multiple disabilities, with the proviso that failure on one item of the developmental scale does not automatically indicate failure on the next, more complex, stage of development.

The constant interactions between child and environment contribute to awareness of co-occurrences. Brinker and Lewis (1982) describe three basic types of co-occurrences or contingencies.

(1) Two events occur together in the individual, such as closing one's eyes and experiencing darkness.
(2) Two events occur together within the environment such as when the child sees his mother and hears vocal sound from her.
(3) An event in the individual occurs with an event in the environment; for example, the child touches a mobile, and the mobile moves.

Contingency awareness is apparent in the child when a different reaction is shown, when an expected co-occurrence does not appear; for example, when a normally noisy rattle is shaken but fails to sound on particular trials. Such contingency awareness is akin to Piaget's secondary circular reactions. Of primary interest in developing contingency awareness in pupils with profound and multiple disabilities are the co-occurrences which involve both the child and the environment, as it is into these instances that teachers and therapists can gain access.

Whatever the nature of the co-occurrence, the fundamental adaptive actions from the child are to detect, associate and remember. Detection of events is dependent firstly on the individual's sensory capacities. Following this, the association of any two events depends on storage in short term memory. Although it has been found that infants under four months of age can associate their movements with a consequent event, if there is a delay of more than three seconds between the infant's movement and the event, even infants as old as nine months fail to link the two (Millar, 1972). The third requirement is the ability to retain a memory or 'scheme' of the occurrences over a long period of time – so that they can be recognised and used when they occur again.

A variety of sources indicate that co-occurrences facilitate an infant's motivational, attentional and cognitive development by orientating the child to his environment, by arousing the interest of the child and by serving as the basis of further mental development.

> Through the operation of memory, they become the elements for subsequent intentions and ultimately for the development of mental structure. (Piaget, 1952)

In their study of the amount and frequency with which mothers and caregivers engaged in talking to and smiling at their infants ('maternal responsiveness'), Lewis and Goldberg (1969) found that 'responsiveness' was related to the infants' perceptual and cognitive development. Infants who received higher levels of 'responsiveness' had significantly higher IQ scores. Other studies such as those of Lewis and Rosenblum (1974), Hartka and Lewis (1981) also support the view that environments rich in co-occurrences contribute to cognitive development.

However, for those with impaired ability to process information from both physical and social environments, and who may also have impairments in motor functioning, engagement with the physical environment is drastically reduced. In addition, parents' expectations of the child may be lowered and styles of interaction changed, resulting in reduced parental responsiveness (Bell, 1980). Handicapped infants clearly shape their parents' behaviour towards them; parental attempts at establishing social contingencies may be extinguished by the absence or irregularity of responding behaviours from their infant. Much of the data on interactions between mothers and normally developing infants, and mothers and handicapped infants, show differences when infants are matched on chronological age, but some of these differences disappear when infants are matched on developmental levels. (Lewis and Wehren, 1982). However, a key factor when learning disabled children are matched on developmental age to normal infants is that they are older and hence the mother has had more time to settle into a particular interactive pattern. The amount of time she has spent with a child with learning disability, who remains at around the same developmental level, may lead her to being less sensitive to signs of development (Brinker and Lewis, 1982) and thus less ready to adopt new sets of expectations and interactive strategies. Jones (1980) also reports several important difficulties in entering into dialogue with the handicapped infant owing to 'vocal clashes' in which both parties vocalise simultaneously, because parents have difficulty in predicting the child's vocal patterns. Other problems can occur because handicapped infants do not tend to look referentially to their mothers after looking at an object, as do normally developing infants. This can make it difficult for parents to establish topics of child initiated interaction.

Such problems can result in parents of handicapped infants taking charge of interactions and providing a greater amount of input than that provided by parents of non handicapped infants of the same age (Buckhalt *et al.*, 1978; Jones, 1980). Parents and caregivers can thus become less and less responsive to the infants' initiations. Such a chain of events, in many instances, can lead to the situation in which only specific activities introduced by the parents lead to predictable patterns of responding:

> The implication is that the behaviour of handicapped infants leads their parents to adopt interactive strategies that ultimately reduce the numbers of contingencies to a few parent-defined situations. This requires the infant to develop a contingency awareness primarily through interactions with objects. (Brinker and Lewis, 1982)

Brinker and Lewis suggest that disabled or impaired infants are particularly likely to be deprived of contingencies because of physical disabilities. Working with non disabled infants at a developmental level of three months, Watson (1972) illustrated the effects of what would be known as 'contingency deprivation' by exposing infants to a situation in which they could not exert control over a rotating mobile. The infants did not subsequently learn to control it when the mobile was later placed under their control. This notion of 'learned helplessness' was developed by Seligman (1975) and Berger and Cunningham (1983), who also suggested that infants with profound learning disabilities were particularly at risk of developing 'secondary motivational handicaps' caused by limited ability to make repetitions of behaviours that cause consequences within the environment. Social co-occurrences are also less likely, as discussed earlier, due to less frequent and weaker social and communicational behaviours. Detection of co-occurrences is impaired by sensory and mental disabilities and, furthermore, parental attempts at interaction may progressively diminish because of the lack of responses from the child (Emde and Brown, 1978; Blacher, 1984).

In summary, development of a generalised expectancy to control the physical or social world is likely to be a problem for the infant with physical disability, sensory impairment or profound learning disability or indeed any combination of the three. The disabled infant is increasingly forced to assume the role of recipient and very rarely that of the initiator. This can lead to increased withdrawal from both physical and social environments which, in turn, leads to further reductions in contingency experiences, apart from those situations defined by others.

The job of the educator of people with profound learning disabilities may be conceptualised as designing and developing an environment that allows the disabled person to cause dramatic change, contingent on specific actions already within the person's repertoire, in order to generate accessible contingencies and, through these, contingency awareness.

The use of microelectronics in promoting establishment of contingency awareness

The amount of research published since 1975 regarding infants and profoundly disabled children and adolescents at early developmental levels is an indication of the increased availability of relatively low-cost microelectronic equipment. Miniaturisation of components has meant that increasingly powerful microelectronic devices have been produced which have become progressively smaller in time and which provide individuals with the opportunity to cause dramatic change in their environments, despite even extensive disabilities.

In 1982, Brinker and Lewis reported on their 'Contingency Intervention Project' which gave learning disabled infants control over environmental events that co-occurred with specific behaviours. They aimed to develop a generalised expectation of control over the environment and an awareness of contingencies. This was accomplished by arranging a variety of consequences on operation of micro switches by means of using actions the child was already capable of making. Eventually, routines of up to 14 behaviours were required to activate the consequence.

Similarly Lovett (1985) produced seven devices to modify the environment, enabling children 'to interact with their surroundings in a meaningful way'. Each piece of equipment gave some form of sensory reinforcement for the target behaviour. The aim of technology was not, he stressed, simply to increase rates of responding, but to develop the child's awareness of his control over aspects of the environment. The equipment included large coloured lights, automatically activated, modified slide projectors and equipment which produced movement for the user, such as a battery powered car in which users would sit and travel on a predetermined path for several seconds. The resulting data from work with adolescents of 14 years of age (at developmental levels not exceeding nine months) was very interesting. It showed that on application of contingent reinforcements, response rates immediately doubled compared to baseline sessions. Perhaps the most important finding from the study was that when tested alone in a quiet environment, the subjects' response rate increased by over one third. This occurred for all individuals in the study.

Similar conclusions were reached by Glenn and Cunningham (1979) and Glenn and Cunningham (1984b). Young children, both disabled and non-disabled, at very early developmental levels, were able to choose which of two auditory stimuli to listen to by touching one of two touch sensitive switches. They concluded that children with profound learning disabilities were active processors of their environments, in ways apparently similar to other children at the same developmental level, and also that they actively sought stimulation when given the chance to do so. They also noted, as others had previously done (Lovett, 1985) that, contrary to the supposed 'spontaneous extinction' phenomenon reported to operate when working with low functioning children (Rice *et al.*, 1967), children with profound learning disability did not show any signs of 'response termination'.

That the systematic use of micro switches in classrooms can contribute to a rich and diverse experience of co-occurrences is not in question. Object based interactions are often the profoundly disabled individual's only reliable experience of contingencies. However, access to micro technology and readily controllable equipment is limited by time and availability. But even when access is unlimited, switches give students experience only of object based interactions. Although some of the equipment mentioned earlier has considerable potential to focus the pupils' attention on their ability to make things happen, it gives no access to person based interaction, which is, after all, the most powerful and direct means of communication and, from this, control (Glenn, 1986).

In our classrooms we often fall into routines of activity to ensure the smooth and efficient management of a class that, while promoting object based interactions, limit pupil initiated dialogues and social co-occurrences The routines of a school community with its attendant structures and timeframes has its drawbacks. We teach in less than sterile conditions and have constant interruptions and routines that often make the transfer of research into the classroom difficult. The numerous daily requirements of passive and active physiotherapy routines, along with ensuring that students are dry and comfortable and at the same time free from thirst and hunger, take up quite a chunk of the working day and available staff time. In addition there are the quite large periods of time required to change students' positions and rotate them through the innumerable pieces of therapeutic positioning equipment that lurk in the room. So how can we strip away these periods of 'dead' time and make as much of the day as possible a contingency rich environment? For example:

Staff/child ratio in Class 6, Melland School
1 teacher, 2 nursery nurses, 1 child care assistant,
10 secondary aged profoundly learning disabled students with additional multiple physical disabilities

Period of required deviation from direct teaching routines
Toileting/changing 3 times a day in class time = 1hr
Drinks for each child twice a day = 1hr 20 mins
Getting pupils' coats on at home time = 0hr 20 mins
(These times represent collective times for listed tasks.)

For this class, staff have lost what is effectively three hours of teaching time through these regular periods of necessary activities whose timings take into account correct and safe lifting techniques as well as the times required for fastening some of the more imaginatively designed harnesses attached to wheelchairs and positioning equipment.

Bearing in mind that the actual teaching time in an average day, when late morning arrivals due to traffic or weather have finally arrived, is in the region of 5 hrs 30 mins, half the day is committed to necessary but time consuming periods where staff are not effectively available to react to, or give consequences to students' attempts at communication or control.

The principles of teaching through contingencies involves working in environments that are responsive to the pupil. Scenarios in which the student has control over objects and people often do not readily make themselves obvious in the working day of the class.

Routines as contingency experience

To ensure a contingency rich environment it is valuable to consider what it must be like to be on the receiving end of a life in a wheelchair, without the access to control that we as empowered adults take for granted. At the start of the day children are awakened and prepared for the routine of the morning; dressed, fed and made ready to be taken to school (often by council transport that might take up to an hour's driving in rush hour traffic). No matter how caring or sensitive the parent or guardian may be, in the rush of the first few hours of the day, time to look closely at the disabled person's body language or affective communication is limited and the indicators of how that person may be feeling may easily be overlooked. As adults, we can easily express states of well being or illness and make decisions about whether we would prefer toast to cereal that morning, or indeed that we do not go out that day at all. We are empowered by our decision making and communication skills unlike the learning disabled child.

Arriving at school, pupils will be taken out of their wheelchairs and manoeuvred or hoisted into changing beds or programmed activities set by teachers and staff eager to make a start on the productive school day. Chances for students to express choices can be minimal. Despite the fact that even the most profoundly learning disabled child has definite preferences which are known by staff, time in which pupils can express those preferences is generally determined by staff when it is most convenient for the management of the whole class, for example individual programme time.

Seligman (1975) identified the existence of 'Secondary Motivational Handicap' present in the lives of many people with profound and multiple learning disabilities (PMLD) and expressed it in terms of a lack of attempts by the person to effect his environment because of the repeated lack of success of previous attempts to control the environment. Similarly Watson (1967) found when dealing with young infants, that once an object (in this case a mobile) was taken out of the immediate control of the child, interest would quickly be lost and attempts at control stopped, even when the mobile was replaced under the child's easy control.

These findings have a definite bearing on classroom practice. Although we anticipate that pupils will learn environmental control through our teaching, the time spent with controllable or micro equipment is less than five per cent of the waking day, and really is not a viable period when put against the rest of what must often (to the learning disabled person) be a chaotic and meaningless day. The fact that the pupils are in the class in the first place indicates that their information gathering systems are limited, and their perception of the day's activity is fundamentally different from ours. Without the ability to form the mental structures required to understand activities around them, our classrooms must often seem totally confusing to our students, who are required to fit in with the activities of the class. How then do we turn this around?

As we find ourselves falling into or creating routines, our students will also have experienced patterns of activity that repeat themselves several times in any day of their lives. Being fed, being changed, having a drink and going into particular rooms (bedroom/class/dining room/school hall, etc.) in which regularly occurring activities take place. Venues and activities are closely linked in our lives and the same is true for our pupils. For instance entry into the cookery room is usually followed by the smells associated with cooking and entry into the bathroom is regularly followed by getting wet. Other routines can be associated with sounds or groups of sounds. Pupils will have heard their name in association with themselves or immediately before activities involving them begin to happen. The concept of ownership of one's name may not be in the pupil's repertoire, but work on the listening preferences of developmentally young pupils by Glenn and Cunningham (1982, 1983, 1984a) indicates that our students may well recognise collections of regularly heard sounds and will pick them out in preference to previously unheard words and dialogue. These normally developing routines are the settings into which teaching staff can bring the principles examined earlier in this chapter into the classroom

To take control effectively we must communicate. To communicate, there must be a **reason** to do so and **content** to transmit. There must also be the **setting conditions** to enable pupils to take control. In the classroom, we must introduce these features into the routines that curiously enough are predominantly those periods of time that were identified earlier as getting in the way of 'teaching'. The so-called dead times.

Routines that have taken years to build, give us potentially prime quality teaching times. Simply by inserting a break in a known routine (setting condition) we give the pupil a reason to communicate, and something to communicate about (content); if, for instance, the pupil is placed on a changing bed and when the changing is finished, staff get into positions that they would normally take to lift him/her up but do nothing. Having been through this routine countless times the pupil will anticipate that he will be lifted from the area to a different place. The fact that something strange is happening to a routine may provoke comment from the child in the form of vocalisation, eye contact with one of the other people involved with the routine or a change in the nature of the child's movement (see, for example, Coupe *et al.*, 1985). Once 'comment' has been passed and acknowledged by the staff, the routine is continued to completion. There are many times in the school day when routines may be used in this way. What is required of staff is to promote communication in the real sense of the word. But situations in which we are promoting child initiated communication require conditions that are specifically oriented to promote motivation. They must also intrinsically carry 'content', or something to be communicated about. A re-evaluation of the dead times often shows them to be potentially the most productive periods of possible activity.

Other examples of opportunities to promote control through communication include the structured disruption of drinking times to promote interaction. The positive or 'like' behaviours frequently displayed by multiply disabled students are often variations on face or eye alignment, opened mouths and other predominantly accepting or passive repertoires. We do not give disliked drinks out of consideration for the feelings of our students. However, reactive behaviours expressing 'not like' are usually more active, noticeable and often more highly motivated expression of affective communication; they are rarely passive. Promoting the 'not like' repertoire, by presenting a disliked drink or food, gives the pupil the chance to completely change a situation into a preferred experience. This outcome of his actions on the environment (changing the drink to the one anticipated) provides a much more noticeable contingency than simple continuation of a session. By empowering students to make noticeable change to their environment, we are helping them to bring it under their control; their environments become places of interest that can be engaged with rather than places of chaotic activity. Drinking and similar pleasurable sessions in the class day can also be used to promote 'turn-taking', 'joint referential looking' and many valuable communication skills.

Glenn and Cunningham (1982; 1984a) found that definite preferences were expressed by children with severe learning disabilities, when they were offered 'motherese' (the simplified code used by caregivers during interactions with their infants) as opposed to the 'elaborate code' of dialogue used by adults when addressing fellow adults. The simplified code is made up of simple repetitive phrases and tonal inflections usually linked to shared activities. While not inferring that the children understood the actual content of the dialogue of the care-giver, Glenn (1986) suggests that the children recognise the patterns of speech. Throughout our lives we are all addressed by our names, and it may be that, of speech patterns used, names would rank highly among recognised sounds. Names are therefore a perfect foundation for a teaching session around which a routine or expectation can be built. The concept of name or the recognition of the significance of its occurrence within the environment is a piece of mutually understood content around which a life long contingency or co-occurrence has occurred. Hearing it is reliably followed by a variety of events that are directly related to the child. A routine is established around which a particular student hears his name spoken in close association with an intrusive but pleasurable consequence, for example, enthusiastic greetings and physical contact of a kind the pupil enjoys. This routine is established over a number of sessions so that the name, consequence and setting of the game are recognised or at least accepted. So called 'sabotage' occurs when at a given time, the pupil's name is called, followed by staff members (who would normally greet the pupil) going to a different member of the group. Having an established routine vary so far from any previous experience has a similar effect on the pupil to that observed in examples discussed earlier.

More importantly for our stated purpose, however, is that it gives staff the opportunity to respond to the 'victim's' notion that the consequence should have involved him. Immediate confirmation of this by staff members makes the pupil's action one of communication. Repeating such sabotage once or twice over a period of two or three weeks in the context of established routines does not, it appears, cause confusion. Indeed orientation to the environment and a heightened degree of arousal results as our pupils begin to realise that they can indeed have control in what was previously an uncontrolled series of events.

The principles of how learning occurs that have been examined and analysed by workers in the field of applied psychology can be used in the classroom once the teachers realise that their role within the class is not one of 'teaching' skills to students with profound and multiple learning disabilities. The teacher should be responsible for the co-ordination and mediation of a responsive environment that has been designed around the needs and behaviours of the pupils.

(b) Teaching Pupils with Profound and Multiple Learning Difficulties to Exert Control

Chris Wilkinson

Rationale

It is difficult to imagine a world such as that which a young person with profound and multiple learning difficulties (PMLD) inhabits and the prison in which he may exist. It is, however, important to start from this point because it offers the chance to acknowledge that this young person, who might be chronologically fourteen years old but intellectually around six months old, has no viable or consistent way of changing or improving his circumstances. Such people are essentially at the mercy of whatever doctrine, ideology or regime that their teachers or carers adopt.

From this perspective it is possible to consider a situation in which pupils are required to perform on demand and without question. They may be able to feed themselves but are never given a choice of food. They may, with aids, be able to walk but never experience freedom of movement around their own classroom. They may be able to build three block towers but are discouraged from conveying 'that's enough'. Certainly they would risk incurring the greatest displeasure if they were ever to convey 'no'!

In the Western world we have travelled along an economic and perhaps even a philosophical path which has led us to judge the worth of an individual by his or her ability to repay debts and accrue wealth (Finch, 1984). We have, it could be argued, pathologised and made deviant those people who most rely upon our integrity to meet their fundamental needs. These are needs which are essential to the emotional and intellectual growth of all people; the need for empowerment, for esteem, for autonomy and for gratifying and pleasurable experiences. Indeed, without returns for these needs we would be prisoners of useless and demeaning lives and would, no doubt, not wish to take an active part in such an existence (Clare, 1990). Young people with PMLD are often accused of being poor participators. Could it be that they very often have no reason to participate? Could it also be that teachers and carers are often guilty of denying them their fundamental needs and that, as a result, they have never been given the opportunity of displaying their true potential?

These are the challenging, exciting and sometimes very provocative issues which have formed the context of curriculum development for pupils with PMLD. The outcome has been a variety of attempts to both deepen our understanding of the human condition and to create environments which offer the PMLD pupil the opportunity to take control.

For any pupil, the possibility of taking control is entrenched in the ability of the educator to perceive 'freedom' as an essential ingredient of curriculum planning and learning experience. The notion of philosophical concepts and theoretical principles which inform a curriculum is not new. In Kelly's book *The Curriculum: Theory and Practice* (1972) he asserts that, in order to educate, rather than train or instruct, the teacher must first identify guiding principles.

Indeed principles should be based on a view of education which offers all pupils the chance of empowerment, esteem and autonomy as well as gratifying and pleasurable experiences. If people are empowered they can make decisions and, as a result, have an impact on their culture, family and community. If they are esteemed and valued for what they are and not for what they might become, they will have status and their views will be taken into account at policy level. In this way they will not be considered to be second rate citizens. If they have autonomy they will gain the skills, knowledge and understanding necessary to give them access to their culture, family and community. If they have gratifying and pleasurable experiences they are more likely to remain intact at an emotional as well as a physical level. It is surely from these principles that we offer an education which is meaningful and relevant. The assertion that more rational decisions about day-to-day teaching can be made is a vision of the future which is 'evocative rather than prescriptive' (Eisner 1969).

Within this context it is essential for those teaching pupils with PMLD to create an atmosphere of continual reflection and enquiry. Daily activities pose questions such as 'Why doesn't John want to join in?', 'How can Nazeem make better use of her locomotive ability?', 'Is the classroom right for Andrew to interact with his environment?', 'Why is Shabeen continually aggressive and withdrawn?'. Finally, there are the implications of such questions for timetabling, resourcing and staff training or awareness. It would, for instance, be impossible to put any principle into practice if the majority of staff were apathetic or antagonistic towards the idea. It would be equally impossible to succeed if the general understanding of 'curriculum' were of education that took place only on-site, in which a particular objective was delivered and assessed in much the same way for every child in the school.

For a variety of reasons the chance for pupils with PMLD to take 'control' is slim. The primary reason for this is that they are often denied those fundamental experiences of the world which promote positive participation. Another reason is that traditionally they have received a product

62

centred curriculum yet it is within the context of a curriculum guided by processes rather than products that they are more likely to experience an education which promotes understanding (McConkey, 1981). Furthermore, it is only within a setting where people are viewed as social beings rather than as being without status that the intellectually honest teaching described by Bruner and Connolly (1974) is likely to take place.

Our aims of curriculum need to be guided by the principles of the Education Act (1989) and the National Curriculum. We must acknowledge that much of the NC content is often far above the ability of pupils with PMLD. However, we endeavour to work within the National Curriculum in a way which will include necessary fundamental experiences, multilateral processes and intellectually honest approaches. These are the ways in which pupils with PMLD will be more likely to 'take control'. Young people who are subjected to methods which adhere to unilateral teaching outcomes which do not include rich and varied experiences and which stress the need for isolatory and clinical settings are unlikely to be able to project themselves upon their environment. They will probably possess a few meagre skills, which they cannot generalise. They will very likely appear uncooperative and disinterested in most aspects of their school lives. They will, in short, be those difficult-to- teach pupils who have a range of bizarre behaviours and about whom it is almost impossible to talk in terms of significant progress (McGee *et al.*, 1987).

The problem is one of conceptualisation and expectation; if people, no matter what their disability, are conceived of as not having the same fundamental human needs as the rest of society, that path may lead to their marginalisation and segregation. Concomitantly, if people are treated as though they will never take control of their environments, that judgement is likely to fulfil itself. We must learn, therefore, to apply the same educational principles to all people, whatever their capacity, and must guard against impeding their progress by adopting attitudes which actually restrict their educational growth (Fraser, 1984).

Checking for the provision of a meaningful and relevant environment

The success of a meaningful and relevant environment will depend upon the ability to adhere to the principles mentioned earlier – offering pupils the chance of empowerment, esteem and autonomy, as well as pleasurable experiences. A way for teachers to ensure that they are continually informing the classroom situation is to assemble a checklist. This list should pick out some of the essential components covering aspects relating to the pupils, the staff, timetabling/curriculum and policy. In this way, it is hoped to establish an overall picture of the situation. It is helpful to check through this list on a regular basis when planning or evaluating work.

Relating to the pupils

(1) Does the pupil appear to be happy/contented?
(2) Does the pupil appear to be able to relate, at own level, to adults and/or events? (Some kind of communication schedule needs to be used here.)
(3) Does the pupil indicate needs or preferences?

Relating to staff

(1) Are staff generally happy and involved with their work?
(2) Is it certain that they have sufficient understanding of what they are trying to achieve? (If staff do not fully understand the rationale, do they behave inappropriately?)
(3) Do staff feel able to discuss the needs of pupils openly with any other member of staff? (Staff who feel confident about their right to make suggestions, question decisions, and act as a member of a team, may behave in quite a different way from those who are unsure of their role or who feel they lack skills for the job.)

Relating to resources

(1) Is there anything that the pupils lack which is severely reducing the quality of their lives?
(2) What activities are the pupils unable to do as a result of lack of resources?
(3) How does this affect their broad and balanced education?

Relating to timetabling/curriculum

(1) Does the structure of the session allow for interaction to take place?
(2) Does the structure of the session allow for a calm, unhurried pace. How?
(3) Are sessions flexible enough? How?
(4) Are sessions challenging? How?
(5) For how much of the day is a pupil given the opportunity of directing rather than being directed?
(6) What was the most enjoyable teaching experience this week? Why?
(7) What might be considered to be the pupil's most enjoyable experience this week? Why?

64

(8) What was the least rewarding teaching experience this week? Why?
(9) What might be considered to be the pupil's least rewarding learning experience this week? Why?

Relating to policies

(1) How visible is the group within the school at the moment?
(2) In which areas, if any, do the pupils appear to suffer from unequal treatment or provision?

Moving on

At first sight, the checklist may appear to be a hotch-potch of unrelated items. In fact, it can serve well in a search for an education which offers freedom, high motivation, and the opportunity to 'grow'. Indeed, pupils who are not yet smiling and who have no positive experience of life can hardly be expected to join in with curriculum objectives; nor are they likely to be able to enter into an autonomous role. Firstly they must experience warmth, trust, anticipation and excitement. Only then will they be ready to experience their world 'solo'.

If pupils are not happy, the idea of forcing a day of 'learning' on them seems absurd. Their immediate need must surely be the alleviation of that distress. In some cases this will be a long and difficult journey, particularly if the pupil is continually aggressive and hostile. But to ignore this and to continue with more pressing curricular matters, is to ignore the fact that there is indeed a teaching situation which requires prior attention. The teacher of a permanently distressed pupil must surely provide a learning environment which will enable him to overcome his problems, to grow in confidence and to build upon reliable relationships.

If the young person does not respond to this approach, the question must surely be, Why? Could the answer lie in the teacher or the environment? (Tomlinson and Barton, 1987). It is important not to assume that the difficulty always lies within the pupil because such an assumption might prevent facing the fact that teachers sometimes cause problems and prolong difficulties, albeit unintentionally.

As for the rest of the checklist, it is important to reiterate the belief that teaching is a multifaceted phenomenon. Its health and success are dependent upon the skilful weaving together of many different features. For example, it is important to consider how special school assistants (SSAs) perceive their job. If SSAs do not feel valued, it is logical to assume that they are likely to have a negative effect upon the teaching situation. Similarly, if the policy of a flexible/interactive learning environment is contrary to the beliefs of other members of staff working within that environment, then getting pupils with PMLD to take control of their lives will surely be much more difficult.

The implication here is for an 'open' teaching situation, in which all members feel a personal investment in the job of teaching. It would, therefore, seem sensible that decisions on lesson planning, teaching targets, school policies and individual problems are not the exclusive concern of the teacher. It is also essential that the views of SSAs should be encouraged and gratefully received by teachers who have a wish to share experiences and grow together (Day *et al.*, 1987). In the search for a situation which offers young people with PMLD the chance to take control, there is a need for a total provision which recognises and accepts that different perceptions do not necessarily infer 'right' or 'wrong', but indicate the need to re-examine the purposes and principles which guide the educational experience in the school (Upton and Cooper, 1990). In other words, young people with profound and multiple learning difficulties are more likely to attain some degree of control if the people who surround them have that capacity themselves.

This discussion has so far been concerned almost exclusively with the responses of the adult world to the condition of the pupil with PMLD. This stems from a strongly held belief that the important issues lie not so much in what is taught but in the way that it is taught. What is more important, that a young person walks from A to B or that he enjoys the experience? That pupils comply with our requests or that they build up communicative structures which allow them to 'negotiate' within the learning experience? Another illustration might be a comparison between punitive attempts to stop aggressive behaviour and the use of strategies which denounce the behaviour rather than the person – the teenager who continually spits may be seen as someone who deliberately rejects all that is offered and gets perverse pleasure from being 'naughty'. This may lead to use of measures which further isolate him, such as 'time-out' or impassioned confrontations in which he is firmly 'told-off'. If the spitting continues and these measures continue to be adopted, to no avail, then it is the pupil who is being denounced. More effective strategies might be to provide experiences which are so supportive and pleasurable that the need to 'reject' is diminished and finally disappears completely (Wood and Shears, 1986).

The environment most likely to ensure that pupils with PMLD become more independent and active is one which is guided by the principle of empowerment, esteem, autonomy and provision of gratifying and pleasurable experiences. Within such an environment it will be possible to construct imaginative, attractive and non-coercive activities. It should also be possible to provide an education which allows the young people to develop qualities such as alertness, friendliness and cooperation which will help to make their participation in the environment much easier (Davis, 1985).

The possibility of pupils with PMLD taking control of their lives depends upon the conviction that they are entitled to the same esteem as any other person. If we hold someone in regard we make sure that their experience of us is as an equal. We pay attention to their thought, wishes and desires. We allow them freedom of thought and movement. We respond to their needs in an empathetic way rather than from a position of personal expediency or desired managerial ease. In this way we support them in their attempts to break out of the prison that is as much our making as theirs. It is hoped that by this means they will emerge into a world of greater opportunities and markedly better prospects.

Chapter Five

Some Implications of the High/Scope Curriculum and the Education of Children with Learning Difficulties

Suzie Mitchell

Introduction

> Children are empowered to carry out self initiated activities as they see fit, unconstrained by the teacher's definition of the correct answer or the correct use of materials . . . Through child initiated learning the child has the opportunity to exert some control over both the learning situation and the teacher. (Weikart, 1989)

This quotation is taken from an address given by David Weikart, the founder and president of the High/Scope Educational Research Foundation in the United States of America (USA). It provides a thumb-nail sketch of the philosophy of the High/Scope Curriculum and, at the same time, shows clearly that the approach is concerned with the locus of control within learning situations. The High/Scope Curriculum has grown out of Weikart's interest in educational disadvantage in relation to social and economic disadvantage, but there are good reasons to take a critical look at the approach and how it may be used or adapted for use with children with learning difficulties.

The High/Scope Curriculum approach

The High/Scope Curriculum is essentially an approach to working with young children and their families, in a nursery or day-care setting. Of central importance is the idea that children learn most effectively when the educational experiences provided are in tune with each child's level of development, are initiated by the child himself and enable the child to reflect his own interests.

The development of the High/Scope Curriculum began in 1961 when Weikart, then Director of Special Education in Michigan, USA, was concerned with whether a good quality pre-school experience could compensate for the problems encountered by children from socio-economically disadvantaged backgrounds. Since then the Curriculum has been, and continues to be, under constant review.

Weikart set up the High/Scope Educational Research Foundation in 1970 in order to undertake research into early childhood education and, specifically, the High/Scope Curriculum and its development. Although Weikart must be acknowledged as the founder of the High/Scope Curriculum, it is important to understand something about the major theoretical influences which lead to, and still underpin, the essential elements of the approach. From the outset the theory of child development as devised by Piaget (1970) has been a major influence. However, the influence of theorists such as Vygotsky (1962), Dewey (1964a and b) and Smilansky (1968) can be identified along with traditional British nursery school practice. If we accept that the High/Scope Curriculum has its roots in established psychological theory and that various aspects of the approach have been subject to empirical research, the essential elements of the approach itself must be outlined in order to set the scene for discussion of the possible uses of the High/Scope Curriculum in the education of children with learning difficulties.

High/Scope is essentially a framework within which children are offered the opportunity to plan some of their experiences within the routine of their day and which provides adults working with those children with a structure within which to do so. It is not a revolutionary new approach to education. It does, however, offer challenges to some teachers to restructure parts of their practice to enable children to take control by initiating some of their own learning experiences.

Elements of the Curriculum

The High/Scope Curriculum can be said to have several essential elements which support the implementation of the Curriculum in two distinct but interrelated ways. Firstly, some of the elements are directly concerned with the way in which the learning space and materials are organised, that is, with the physical environment in which the children learn. Secondly, and in many ways more importantly, some elements of the High/Scope Curriculum directly address the role of the adult as a facilitator of a variety of active and interactive learning opportunities; child to child, adult to child, child to adult, child to materials and child to environment.

The main elements of the approach are considered to be Active learning and the Plan–do–review sequence. To complement these and place them in context, further elements are identified. These are Room arrangement, Tidy up time, Small group time, Large group time, Key experiences and Parental involvement.

Active learning

This has already been cited as one of the cornerstones of the approach. It is seen as a process by which children explore their world, a natural process that cannot be imposed by adults. All classroom activities should include the ingredients of active learning and one of the roles of the adult is to create the conditions necessary for this to take place. Five basic ingredients which must be present for active learning to occur are:

- Materials: a variety of interesting materials must be available and readily accessible to the children.
- Manipulation: children must be free to work with the materials, to handle them and explore their properties.
- Choice: children must have the opportunity to decide what they want to do, to select their own materials and activities.
- Language: communication, or talk from the children, must be acknowledged as being of value (as they share their experiences of what they have done or what they are doing).
- Adult support: adults are instrumental in encouraging the children's efforts and in helping them to build on their skills by joining in with their play and by helping them to solve problems as they arise.

Active learning includes activities such as looking and observing, listening, touching and handling, smelling, moving and searching and making things happen in the world around. Children's knowledge and understanding of the world comes from personal interaction with real things, including people, within their environment. The role of the adult is therefore to enable and encourage these experiences. Hence teachers must be committed to providing opportunities for active learning.

It has been suggested that within this Curriculum the role of the adult is less clear than in more traditional educational settings where the teacher decides what the children will experience and learn. First and foremost the adult is seen as a facilitator of a child's active learning. The adult is also the administrator of the various aspects of the High/Scope Curriculum within which children are involved in child initiated, active learning. The adult is seen as a partner in the child's learning rather than a controller of it and guides the child through broad-ranging developmental milestones, known as 'Key Experiences', while continuously monitoring the level of development. The adult is expected to become actively involved in the children's activities, listening closely to their plans, working with them and presenting challenges to extend their awareness and understanding of what they are doing. The adult is also to be aware of the role of supportive communication strategies, particularly that of 'open' questions (questions to which there is more than one answer). This style of questioning enables the adult to gain information from the child, allows insight into the child's understanding of what he is doing and offers opportunities to enter the child's own level of play or work rather than the level at which the adult assumes the child to be operating. Through open questioning the adult and the child can interact co-operatively, as equals, in the child's chosen task without the risk of the adult taking over the activity. By engaging with individual children at their own level, the adult is in a unique position to understand each child's skills and interests and monitor progress. The role of the adult in the High/Scope Curriculum is, if anything, more demanding than the role which requires her to do all the planning and deciding before the children arrive at school. The approach demands letting go of the planning and deciding and spending time instead working with the children, using the special knowledge gained to understand each child's level of development, and subsequently utilising opportunities to challenge and extend the child's skills. One of the strengths of the High/Scope Curriculum approach, as the remaining elements clarify, is that it provides concrete guidance on how to accomplish these somewhat awesome tasks.

Daily routine (Plan–do–review)

Beyond the role of the adult and the concept of active learning, is the daily routine; as far as enabling the child to take some control of his learning is concerned, this is the core of the High/Scope approach. A stable daily routine provides children with a secure learning environment in which they can learn to predict the sequence of events in their day.

The sequence of Plan–do–review is the specific element which allows children to make choices about what they are going to do and at the same time allows the teacher to remain involved in that process. In order to understand the importance of the sequence as a whole, each part can be considered in its own right.

(1) **Planning time** This is when children are encouraged to think about what they are going to do. As has been stated by proponents of the High/Scope approach (Schweinhart, 1988), children make choices and

decisions all the time but are rarely required to think about these decisions in a systematic way or to realise the possibilities and consequences which relate to the choices they make. Within High/Scope each child is enabled to express his ideas to an attentive adult who is poised, if necessary, to help realise the plan. Through this the child has the opportunity to view himself as a person, not only capable of making plans or choices but also as someone worth being listened to. Ideally planning-time should also include the child's peers.

During planning time both the child and the adult are seen to be of equal importance and, as such, both benefit. The child is supported and ready to employ his plan while the adult has a clear idea of what the child intends to do and where he may need help. The child, while expressing ideas or plans, has the chance of forming an internal image before carrying them out. The adult has another opportunity to assess the child's level of development and interests.

(2) **Work time** Once the child has made a plan he then has the opportunity of carrying it out through a daily routine known as Work time. This is an active and busy part of the day for both the child and the adult and can pose problems for adults new to working with the Curriculum. It is within this part of the daily routine that the adult must resist the temptation to either take over the lead or withdraw from the child's activity. During Work time the child is implementing his plan while the adult observes and enters into the activity in order to help, encourage, extend and share each child's experiences.

(3) **Recall time** When the child has finished with the completed activity, encouragement is given to look back over what has been done and to relate that to the original plan. This is the final part of the Plan–do–review sequence. It is referred to as Recall time and brings to a close the child's Planning and Work time activities. The adult's role during Recall time is to help children make a link between what they planned to do and what they actually did.They are also helped to represent their Work time experiences. This can be done in whatever way their developmental level allows, through speech, drawing, bringing a toy to the review session, looking towards an area of the classroom or by indicating a friend with whom they worked – to mention just five possibilities.

Criticism of the High/Scope Curriculum approach has mainly focused on the Plan–do–review sequence, particularly the review aspect where concern has been expressed over the use of the word 'review'. This has resulted in a debate over the true meaning of the word and whether what occurs in High/Scope is review, recall or reflection (Jordan and Powell, 1990). This may be a valid debate in terms of semantics but enabling the child to look back over what he has done and helping him to link that in with the original plan is what is felt to be important – whatever it is called.

Room arrangement

The arrangement of the classroom is of special importance in High/Scope. All the materials, toys and equipment intended for the children's use are readily available on open shelves, and at child height. All are clearly labelled, in a form that the child can understand, to enable the children to become involved in the next element.

Tidy up time

Tidy up time occurs between Work time and Recall time. Children are expected, and helped, to return whatever they have been working or playing with to the place to which it belongs. They are also encouraged to store incomplete projects, for completion during another session. Tidy up time draws Work time to a close, aiming to foster a sense of responsibility in the children. It is another opportunity for adults and children to work together.

Small group time

Small group time represents the time when the teacher, using the information gained about the children during previous sessions, presents an activity in which they participate for a set period of time. The activity is structured by the teacher but the children's actions and responses follow no predetermined sequence. They are encouraged to explore the materials offered, to use their senses, ask questions, make choices and decisions, solve problems and to work with both the adult and other children. The adult not only sets up the activity but also responds to the children's needs in terms of their abilities, interests and problems.

Large group time

Large group time is when the whole group meets together, often at the beginning of the day as well as at the end of a session, to sing, play games or perhaps listen to a story. This element gives children the opportunity to join in and learn to function as a member of the whole group, sharing and learning from their peers.

Key experiences

The Key experiences represent the structure around which each child's developmental progress is reviewed. They are a way of helping the teacher to focus on the child's level of development and thus support the child in extending his experiences. The Key experiences are categorised into nine areas: Use of language, Representation of experiences, Classification, Seriation number concepts, Spatial relations, Time, Movement, Social and Emotional. These main areas are each sub-divided further into types of experiences. It is important to note that the Key experiences are not mutually exclusive and that any one learning activity may involve more than one. The system of recording within the High/Scope Curriculum is primarily one of anecdotal notes, on a specially designed recording form, on which is recorded those experiences observed to have occurred, within the Key experiences. Being different to the check list type of recording, this method serves to remind us that it is what a child can actually demonstrate he can do that is important; that teaching does not necessarily lead to learning.

Parental involvement

Parental involvement is seen as a vital aspect of the High/Scope Curriculum approach. In the USA for instance, home visiting has always been included. It is necessary to acknowledge the interrelationship of the roles of the child's parents and teachers. A belief that both parents and teachers are expert within their mutual roles of child care and development is essential for this Curriculum to be successful.

By continually evolving and developing the High/Scope Curriculum is able to respond to changes in educational thought. 'The program is, of course, not complete; it never can be, because the society in which our children grow is constantly changing and education must respond to change' (Hohmann, Banet & Weikart, 1979).

High/Scope and children with learning difficulties

Given that the High/Scope Curriculum was originally devised for socio-economically disadvantaged pre-school children in America, how relevant is it for children with learning difficulties in schools in Britain? The proponents of the approach profess its adaptability to changing circumstances and Tompkins (1991) of the High/Scope Educational Research Foundation argues that the approach is highly relevant for children with learning difficulties.

Members of the Warnock Committee (DES, 1978) were of the opinion that 'the aims of education are the same, whatever the advantages or disadvantages of the boy or girl concerned'. Two primary aims were stated. Firstly that education should increase children's knowledge of the world they live in and their imaginative understanding, both of the possibilities of that world and their own responsibilities in it. Secondly that education should give a child as much independence and self-sufficiency as he is capable of, by teaching those things that must be known 'in order to find work and to manage and control his life'.

This emphasis on education being concerned with a child being able to 'manage and control his life' is gathering momentum in the arena of special educational needs. For children with severe and moderate learning difficulties it might be viewed as a somewhat novel approach. However, growing interest in the use of interactive approaches in the education of children with learning difficulties is reflected in recent publications; see for example, Ashman and Conway (1989), Smith (1991). Interaction is, as McConkey (1988) has stated 'the forum in which the infant achieves his earliest skills . . . much of what constitutes an interactive learning approach may be little different in practice from what the proverbial "good" teacher or parent does intuitively'. He goes on to indicate 'we should be under no illusion how radically different this approach is to the prescriptive methods which have been most vigorously promulgated in special education'. Based on the theory of learning described by Skinner (1968) the behavioural approach has enjoyed application in classrooms, in particular those for children with severe learning difficulties. It is concerned with the observable behaviour of the learner, and control over what is to be taught. How it is to be taught and whether it has been learned to an acceptable level, is in the hands of the teacher. It has certainly had its place, being used by teachers who were then able to show evidence of children's learning. Considering that until 1971 children with severe learning difficulties had been officially considered ineducable, this was an important step. The behavioural approach worked! It gave the children measurable increases in their level of skills – quickly. Through this approach, pupils could be taught skills that they would not necessarily have learned spontaneously. Teachers could demonstrate that they had taught the child the skills in question and, maybe most importantly, a framework for teaching could be followed that was seen to be embedded in a theory of learning. It gave a sense of security.

The behavioural approach had its place in the education of children with learning difficulties and in certain circumstances still does. Teaching, indeed life, is not a 'black and white' or 'all or nothing' affair and one approach cannot be adopted to the exclusion of all others. However, the education of children with learning difficulties has to keep pace with new thinking on how learning takes place. The High/Scope Curriculum approach offers a framework within which to do this. Behavioural theorists consider learning to take place as a result of practice, repetition of an act or action causing a biological alteration in the learner which enables the learner to carry out that action again. The traditional behavioural approach to learning does not acknowledge any internal mental aspects of the learner and does not therefore necessarily require that the learner is consciously involved. The approach has tended to encourage teachers to see pupils as passive and not actively involved in the learning process. The teacher appears to have ultimate control over all aspects of the learning process. Now however, there is a growing belief that for learning to take place, the learner has to be actively involved in the process. Tomlinson (1989) argues that the acquisition of skills involves more than simple practice and provides an analysis which fits into the Plan–do–review element of the High/Scope Curriculum approach.

Skills, according to Tomlinson, can be seen as anything that a person can do; from riding a bicycle, to reading, to thinking. A skill is something we have learned. Learning is seen as an active process which involves cognitive processing skills. These cognitive processing skills include attending to selected detail holding information in a working memory, comparing new information with that held in a long term memory, generating a plan of action (Plan), implementing this plan (Do) and using feedback (Review) to see if the plan worked. All this implies positive action on the part of the learner. If a person is actively involved in an activity there must be some degree of control being exerted by that participant, even if the only form of control he can exercise is to stop! The High/Scope Curriculum approach, with its emphasis on active learning and the sequence of Plan–do–review, would seem to be of value in the education of children with learning difficulties in order to extend and enhance the degree of control children have over their own learning. Tomlinson has provided a link between the process of learning and the Plan–do–review of the High/Scope Curriculum.

It has been stated that little progress can be made by maintaining what can be seen as an artificial distinction between behavioural and cognitive approaches (Smith, 1989) and that the two can work together. The High/Scope Curriculum is one such example where aspects of the behavioural approach to learning can work alongside and within an interaction-based or cognitive framework. There are aspects of the High/Scope Curriculum which would plainly have to be adapted for use in some settings and for use with some children. However, it is important not to get too 'hung up' on these and appreciate that it is acceptable to adapt and apply. Certainly the word 'plan', so essential to the High/Scope Curriculum and to the idea of having some control over one's life, could be seen as an obstacle to the implementation of the High/Scope Curriculum for children with special educational needs. There will be many children currently being educated in schools for children with learning difficulties and some in mainstream schools who would not be able to plan in the ordinary sense of the word. Within the notion of 'adapt and apply' it is suggested that the concept of 'to plan' can be broken down into a developmental sequence. This might begin around facilitating the process of choice and end with the child being able to develop a plan. Similarly there may be problems connected to the word 'interaction'; something intrinsic to the High/Scope Curriculum approach. Again, there are children who pose great challenges when it comes to facilitating interaction with their environment as well as with their peers and teachers. Longhorn (1988) has addressed this question by describing a developmental sequence for interactive learning which involves elements such as co-active learning, co-operative learning, reactive learning and preference learning. This sequence too, could be utilised for the interaction required by the High/Scope Curriculum approach. Similarly, other aspects of the High/Scope approach that will require adaptation for use in the child's own setting can be considered. However, in adapting elements of the framework offered by the High/Scope Curriculum, the fundamental commitment to child initiated learning must not be masked – or what is being offered can no longer be called High/Scope.

In the UK, it is important to acknowledge that access to the National Curriculum is every child's right between 5 and 16 years of age. How then does the High/Scope Curriculum fit in with this, given that it was devised more than 25 years before the advent of the National Curriculum, originally for use in America and primarily for use with pre-school children? This question has been addressed by High/Scope UK (Brown, 1991) and Warwickshire County Council (1989). The result has been publications which outline how well the High/Scope Curriculum leads children into the National Curriculum and also how High/Scope Key experiences cover many aspects of the National Curriculum attainment targets at the early levels. A child learning within the High/Scope Curriculum Key experiences would be experiencing the broad and balanced curriculum demanded by the legislation up to and including Level One of the attainment targets in the core subjects of the National Curriculum. As the High/Scope Educational Research Foundation is now extending its interest beyond the pre-school years, it will be interesting to see whether this aspect (known as 'K through 3') continues to enhance work within the National Curriculum.

The extension of the High/Scope Curriculum beyond the pre-school years with the 'K through 3' materials (High Scope, 1991), and the arguments put forward by Dennison and Kirk (1990) for the role of experiential learning in adult education, encourage exploration of the use of the High/Scope Curriculum with older children and adults. Dennison and Kirk provided adult students of average learning ability with active learning experiences. They describe a cycle of Plan–Review–Learn–Apply and stress the importance of holistic, humanistic or active learning which highlights the need to focus on the individual learner, rather than on the material to be learned. Warning against the dangers of 'didacticism' they argue that a teacher possesses certain skills or knowledge to impart to the learner but that if learning activities are not initiated by the learner there is a risk of attempting to 'provide answers when questions have not even been asked'. While teachers help to formalise, accelerate and focus the learning process, they cannot control it. Learning, they insist, is always internal to the learner and therefore beyond the control of the teacher, whose main task is to guide the learner round the learning cycle. Teachers do have control over the experience in that they offer a clear framework for the 'Do' part of the cycle, they can also help to motivate and support the learner at any part of the cycle. The deliberate construction of such learning cycles, argue Dennison and Kirk, provides for experiential learning.

Views held on how learning takes place, together with those on child development, are fundamental to the way a teacher will teach. These views will determine how attractive the High/Scope Curriculum appears on initial acquaintance. Those who agree that 'we should be looking for ways of helping young people to become more active partners in the learning process' (Knight, 1991) are the most likely to be attracted to it. The High/Scope Curriculum unquestionably needs to be the subject of critical empirical research within the field of the education of children with learning difficulties. It is felt to be worthy of such study in the light of current theories of learning and growing frustrations with behavioural approaches. It could provide a useful and coherent framework within which teachers allow their pupils to take a degree of control over their learning – and thereby, their lives.

[**Note**: The views expressed in this chapter are not necessarily those held by the High/Scope Institute UK or the High Scope Educational Research Foundation. They are personal to the author.]

Chapter Six

Teaching as Dialogue: Teaching Approaches and Learning Styles in Schools for Pupils with Learning Difficulties

Richard Byers

It's been a long time coming ...

It is interesting to note that teachers in mainstream schools have often viewed the National Curriculum, with its structured assessment arrangements built around hierarchies of Attainment Targets, as a restrictive influence. Teachers in schools for pupils with learning difficulties are only too familiar with a curriculum which is driven by prescriptive and constraining assessment procedures. For them the National Curriculum may be seen in a very different light. The redefinition of the whole curriculum, the explicit references to personal and social education and the acknowledgement, in statute, of the significance of a range of teaching approaches and learning styles may be seen as a force for liberation and as a means by which pupils with learning difficulties may be encouraged to take control. This chapter, which begins with some reflections about the education of pupils with severe learning difficulties, seeks to contribute to this general debate.

In 1970, when responsibility for the learning needs of pupils with severe learning difficulties was given to schools, teachers were faced with a new challenge. The Junior Training Centres had offered care, occupation and a training in life skills. Schools, however, need to offer an education. Teachers operating in something of a theoretical vacuum turned to psychologists and to the theory and practice of behaviourism for guidance and inspiration. In adopting a behaviourally-orientated, checklist-driven model for the education of pupils with severe learning difficulties, teachers accepted hypotheses which were presented as *a priori* truths. I remember, for instance, my training in behaviour modification techniques. An assessment and teaching system originally designed for use with pre-school American children was presented to groups of teachers as the way forward for English pupils of all ages who experienced severe learning difficulties. The psychologists who trained teachers in the use of the system encouraged the setting of precise objectives within individual pupil programmes. Objectives which could not be verified behaviourally were to be avoided. Teachers were offered the A B C model – Antecedents leading to Behaviour followed by Consequences – as a way to conceptualise the learning process. They were told that by shaping the antecedents (getting the conditions right) and controlling the consequences (rewards and sanctions) they would be able to modify behaviour and pupils would learn. Learning was said to occur most effectively when objectives were broken down into small steps by task analysis. Pupils were thereby taught logically-sequenced chains of small sub-skills which would build incrementally into whole new skills. If this sounded simplistic the trainers added a little obfuscation in the form of recommendations about managing the situations in which this form of learning took place (usually, for example, in distraction-free or restricted environments) and about ways of recording success or failure against established criteria (including whether or not the pupil required any form of prompt in order to complete the task successfully). The psychologists told the teachers that all human behaviour could be analysed and manipulated in this way and that there was really nothing else that they needed to know about the learning requirements of pupils in the newly-established schools for pupils with severe learning difficulties.

I remember that training. I remember leaving the sessions, my checklist and teaching cards under my arm, with a sense that I now knew what I was doing. I was not then aware of how much contentious baggage I was taking away along with my checklist. I had a sense that my sixties liberal romanticism was offended by the idea that all human behaviour could be reduced to A B C – all human behaviour? – but managed to tuck this away in the back of my mind since the rest of the package seemed so appealing to a teacher who was floundering among the responsibilities of a new job. Here was a system which confidently and authoritatively told me what to do. Here was something I could start with my class next week. Here was something that the school wanted to adopt as its chosen system. No-one else seemed to be proposing an alternative system.

So behaviourism it was, for a while at least. I filled in activity charts, setting objectives against performance criteria and recording the successes and failures and prompts. I completed checklists and offered rewards. I taught in my one-to-one corner and subjected pupils to 'time out' when their behaviour became unacceptable. And my pupils made progress. At least, they made progress in certain areas. It was possible to apply backward chaining techniques very successfully, to putting on a sock. It was even possible to persuade pupils to look towards you if you held a sweet in front of your face and popped it into their mouths when their eyes met yours. But I, like many other teachers, began to question the idea that this represented a complete model of the teaching and learning process.

... but I know a change *is* gonna come

It was a pupil who finally brought me to question the hypothesis that behavioural psychology represented the last word on the subject of learning. I had been trying to toilet-train Mary for months and was beginning to have some success. Mary liked my guitar playing. It seemed to relax her enough to enable her to let go, as it were. So I had taken to playing Mary a tune as she sat on her potty. We were having some success but the Educational Psychologist knew that my methods were unorthodox. He undertook to train Mary for me and disappeared into the toilet area with Mary, some charts, a stop watch and a bag of sweets. He persevered for quite some time but Mary did not approve of this regime. She clearly resented being separated from the group for long periods of time and shut up in the toilet with a stranger, even if he did have a never-ending supply of sweets. Mary withheld her urine and cried. She persevered for quite some time until the Educational Psychologist went away with his blank charts, his stop watch and his sweets and Mary was able to rejoin her pals. I got the guitar out again and went back to being unorthodox and approximate.

I tell this story in detail because I believe that it is, in its small way, profoundly instructive and because I am indebted to Mary, who incidentally became a fully continent music-lover, for its lesson. Mary's toilet training did not, in the end, depend upon a simple mechanistic view of behaviour. It depended upon social relationships, upon Mary's mood, upon whether she felt happy and relaxed. It was actually a complex phenomenon. It depended upon me taking account of who Mary was as a person. Could I have translated this into behavioural lore? 'Happy' and 'relaxed' are, of course, problematic concepts for behaviourists. How could they be quantified? 'Place Mary on the potty. Ensure that she is smiling and refraining from biting her nails'? I doubt whether this approach would have had any more success than the stop watch and sweets. I came to rely instead upon a degree of intuition and leavened the dough of my precision teaching with a healthy measure of humanity, as, of course, did many teachers of children with severe learning difficulties.

What was the nature of the baggage that I had taken away uncritically from those behaviour modification training sessions? What was it that Mary encouraged me to re-examine? Looked at superficially, objectives-orientated, behavioural systems are primarily about checklists. In other words they define the content of the curriculum by indicating, at all times, the next step to take. They suggest a rolling process of assessment (colour in the checklist), followed by the setting of objectives (look for the next empty box on the checklist), followed by teaching (*half shade* that box on the checklist – 'I am working on this'), followed by more assessment (colour in the checklist again). Some schools for pupils with severe and moderate learning difficulties appear to have absorbed the National Curriculum in exactly this spirit, seeing the Attainment Targets as a glorified checklist, ripe for task analysis. There is some doubt as to whether this is an entirely appropriate way to engage with the National Curriculum, but that is the subject of a slightly different debate (see Sebba and Byers, 1992). For the purposes of this chapter it is enough to acknowledge that many teachers do like to adopt a checklist as a definition of curriculum content.

It should not be forgotten, however, that the contentious baggage which accompanied the original behavioural checklists also prescribed a far broader territory for teachers. The accepted wisdom of behavioural theory also defined teaching method and the nature of learning itself. It stated that teaching is a precise science; that it should pursue predetermined objectives defined by assessment hierarchies and that it works best when there is a one-to-one relationship between teacher and pupil. Learning, according to the accepted wisdom, follows separate, developmentally preordained, neatly sequenced paths and occurs preferably under clinically controlled circumstances, when the rewards are right. In other words, the best learning takes place when a single objective is pursued by a teacher shaping the behaviour of an individual pupil.

Teachers, over the years, became aware of the shortcomings of the systems operated within schools for pupils with severe learning difficulties. Much of the dissatisfaction focused upon the checklists themselves (they were never detailed enough, were they?) and resulted in a constant search for a new, more perfect, checklist. Some brave souls also began to challenge the methodological dominance of behavioural thought and surreptitiously to modify behaviour modification. It was difficult, however, to let go of the checklists. The problem was that there was no system with which to replace them and no access to a reputable special educational theory with which to challenge behaviourism. Some pioneering spirits were undeterred and set off down their own route anyway, see for instance

McGee, Menolascino, Hobbs and Menousek's (1987) *Gentle Teaching,* the contributions to *Interactive Approaches to the Education of Children with Severe Learning Difficulties* (Smith, 1988) and Nind and Hewett (1988) in *Interaction as Curriculum.* As a result, challenging new positions were carved out for teachers involved with pupils with severe learning difficulties. But the introduction of the National Curriculum has set the issues in a broader context and requires teachers in schools for pupils with learning difficulties to engage with the current discussion about teaching approaches and learning styles alongside their colleagues in mainstream schools.

Balance and variety

The introduction of the National Curriculum represents, in many ways, a revolution as profound in its implications as the legal acceptance in 1970 of the 'educability' of pupils with severe learning difficulties. The Education Reform Act of 1988 places a statutory responsibility upon all schools to provide a broad and balanced curriculum which 'promotes the spiritual, moral, cultural, mental and physical development of pupils' and which 'prepares pupils for the opportunities, responsibilities and experiences of adult life'. *Curriculum Guidance 3 – The Whole Curriculum* (NCC ,1990a) states that 'the National Curriculum alone will not provide the necessary breadth' and defines a whole curriculum which includes the core and other foundation subjects of the National Curriculum (the 'basic curriculum'); religious education; 'additional subjects beyond the 10 subjects of the National Curriculum'; 'an accepted range of cross-curricular elements'; and 'extra-curricular activities'. So far the definition explores a vision of curricular content which in itself may be seen as liberating for schools for pupils with severe and moderate learning difficulties (see, for example, Ashdown *et al.,* 1991). But *Curriculum Guidance 3* (NCC, 1990a) goes further. It describes the 'intangibles which come from the spirit and ethos of each school' together with consideration of the 'most effective teaching methods' and the 'efficient and imaginative management of the curriculum and of the school' as also being part of the whole curriculum. There is not space here to debate the impact upon the whole curriculum of spirit and ethos nor of management strategies, profoundly significant though these factors clearly are (see Sebba, Byers and Rose, 1993). Consider, however, the phrase 'the most effective teaching methods' and its implication that no single methodology can provide a complete response to pupils' learning requirements.

If you had taken account of some of the voices which have been raised recently, you might have begun to feel that there is only one ministerially approved way to teach. Consider the following scenario:

'Ere. Miss,what's this?' (*Dead butterfly is offered up to teacher's attention on a small palm.*)

There is a pause in the babble of the mixed ability class of nine-year-olds. It is as if the children, like the teacher, sense the pivotal nature of this moment.

'It's a dead butterfly, Shane,' says the teacher. 'Dispose of it hygienically then sit down and be quiet. It is time for this week's mental arithmetic test.'

This excerpt encapsulates a philosophy which brooks no floppy liberal nonsense about childish curiosity or spontaneity or pupil-led learning or topic work (compare with the original in Byers, 1992). This time Shane's teacher has her priorities sorted out. She is following a prescribed curriculum. She is filling her pupils with knowledge and testing them regularly to make sure none of it has leaked out again. She is teaching; the pupils are learning; she is conducting teacher assessment on a continuous basis. She is firmly in control. Is this the kind of education which is prescribed by a National Curriculum and a national programme of assessment arrangements? Is this what *Curriculum Guidance 3* means when it states that consideration of the 'most effective teaching methods' should be seen as part of whole curriculum planning? A later paragraph in the same document suggests not:

> The Education Reform Act does not prescribe how pupils should be taught. It is the birthright of the teaching profession, and must remain so, to decide on the best and most appropriate means of imparting education to pupils. If the whole curriculum is to mean anything then it must be imparted by use of a wide range of teaching methods, formal and informal, class and group, didactic and practical. The wide range of skills which pupils must acquire must be reflected in an equally wide variety of approaches to teaching.

The National Curriculum Council is not alone in commending to teachers a variety of teaching methods. The authors of the recent discussion paper concerning *Curriculum Organisation and Classroom Practice in Primary Schools* (Alexander *et al.*, 1992) endorse 'the common-sense view that teachers need to be competent in a range of techniques in order to achieve different learning outcomes'. They go on to delineate the territories which this 'range of techniques' should cover. They argue for 'an appropriate balance of subject and carefully focused topic work' which will 'preserve the integrity of each subject' and 'ensure an appropriate balance of the various cross-subject activities'. They encourage teachers to provide learning tasks which enable pupils to 'engage in creative and imaginative thinking and action' in addition to consolidating, practising and extending their existing skills, knowledge and understanding. They suggest that classroom practice will be more effective if teachers use a variety of deliberate strategies for grouping pupils including 'collaborative group work' in addition to 'whole class teaching, group teaching and one-to-one work with individuals'.

Put succinctly, Alexander, Rose and Woodhead (1992) are advocating balance and variety. They suggest that there is a need to offer integrated studies as well as subject specific lessons; investigative problem-solving learning opportunities as well as didactic teaching; co-operative group activity as well as individual or whole class tuition. This appears to challenge the advice of the behaviourists in at least three fundamental ways. Behavioural philosophy was characterised earlier in this chapter as proposing that the best learning takes place when a single objective is pursued by a teacher shaping the behaviour of an individual pupil. It is suggested here that cross-subject activities will necessarily present a more complex matrix of learning opportunities than can be contained in the notion of 'a single objective'. It is also suggested that 'creative and imaginative thinking and action' on the part of pupils cannot take place while pupil behaviour is viewed as requiring 'teacher shaping'. Finally, it is suggested that 'collaborative group work' is impossible where a one-to-one relationship exists between teacher and pupil. A more sophisticated analysis of the teaching and learning process than can be accommodated in a system which advocates the tutoring of individual pupils in predetermined, isolated skills is presented by these 'three wise persons'.

These suggestions, of course, beg a number of questions. Alexander, Rose and Woodhead are, after all, talking about mainstream, primary phase education. Do their conclusions apply also to schools for pupils with severe and moderate learning difficulties? If so, do such schools have to abandon their reliance upon objectives-based teaching methods? The answer to the second question is 'no'. The three wise persons argue for balance and variety and this balance and variety will include tightly focused, skills orientated, one-to-one teaching. The adoption of behavioural methodology represented an important step in the evolution of teaching pupils with learning difficulties. It facilitated, to coin a phrase, a great leap forward and still has a great deal of value to offer. It is suggested that another important stage has now been reached in the evolutionary process and that an opportunity exists for teachers in schools for pupils with learning difficulties to expand their horizons and to realise the ideal of a whole curriculum which meets the needs of all pupils in all schools.

Inside the National Curriculum

The National Curriculum is proclaimed as a curriculum for all. Most of the debate about the validity of this claim has focused upon the content of the

National Curriculum core and other foundation subjects. Undoubtedly this debate will continue. The resulting modifications to the subject orders and to the statutes defining their implementation and assessment will, it is hoped, continue to lead towards a curriculum which is truly accessible to all pupils. But the National Curriculum, as *Curriculum Guidance 3 – The Whole Curriculum* (NCC ,1990a) makes clear, is about more than subject content. The subject orders themselves contain many messages about teaching approaches and learning styles. It is not possible to implement the subject content of the National Curriculum without entering into the methodological debate. A few examples may elucidate the issues

Curriculum Guidance 3 – The Whole Curriculum states that 'the full potential of the 10 subjects will only be realised if, in curriculum planning, schools seek to identify the considerable overlaps which exist both in content and in skills'. The document goes on to suggest that 'interdisciplinary sharing of the teaching of programmes of study', or the creation of schemes of work which integrate the subjects, will allow schools an opportunity to capitalise upon these deliberate links between subjects. The practicalities of this sort of integrated approach are discussed in detail in the section 'Exploring Inter-Subject Links' in *Curriculum Guidance 9 – The National Curriculum and Pupils with Severe Learning Difficulties* (NCC, 1992) and in Byers (1992).

Even a cursory glance at the programmes of study for the core and other foundation subjects at Key Stage 1 will reveal large areas of common territory. The notion of handling data appears in both the science (DES, 1991d) and the mathematics orders (DES, 1991c) for instance. Sorting, grouping and classifying skills are required in mathematics and sciences, also in geography (DES, 1991a) for example, the requirement to identify similarities and differences between places, 'eg in the ways land and buildings are used and in the life and work of people', and in history (DES, 1991b) 'distinguish between different versions of events, eg different accounts by pupils of events which happened in the school a week, month or year ago'. The use of stories as a medium for subject exploration is advocated in history and in geography, while the link with English (DES, 1989) as a subject is obvious.

Many Local Education Authorities have used the links between subjects as a rationale for encouraging interdisciplinary planning and integrated implementation at Key Stages 1 and 2. Some schools are looking at integrated planning in Key Stages 3 and 4, as recommended in *Curriculum Guidance 3*. Increasingly, the non-statutory guidance provided by the National Curriculum Council emphasises the links between subjects. For instance, non-statutory guidance for information technology (NCC, 1990b) employs the concept of 'strands' such as 'Communicating Information', 'Handling Information' and 'Measurement and Control' to show ways in which the subjects interrelate. Clearly echoes of these ideas will be found in other subject documents – in English, science and mathematics, for example. The non-statutory guidance goes on to emphasise the need to ensure that 'IT capability is delivered not in isolation but across the curriculum'. In a section entitled 'Developing IT Capability in Foundation Subjects', examples are given, across all the Key Stages, of ways in which information technology may contribute both to the teaching of other discrete subjects and to the planning of 'themes' or integrated schemes of work. The non-statutory guidance for mathematics (NCC,1989) contains a whole section which deals with cross-curricular approaches and activities. Cross-curricular planning is discussed and examples provided of ways in which 'mathematical activity can contribute significantly to the development of more general skills such as communicating, reasoning and problem-solving'. Finally, the *Curriculum Guidance* documents devoted to a detailed exposition of the cross-curricular themes offer numerous examples of the ways in which learning opportunities in relation to the core and other foundation subjects may be offered in the context of integrated, thematically-conceived schemes of work. *The Curriculum Guidance* documents 4–8 (NCC, 1990 c – g) all make these cross-subject links explicit. *Curriculum Guidance 4 – Education for Economic and Industrial Understanding* , provides particularly clear and thorough plans for cross-curricular activity for pupils of all ages.

Many National Curriculum Council publications advance the notion of cross-curricular planning but there is more to the philosophy of thematic work than the mere integration of subjects for the sake of efficient management. Proponents of the topic approach have, traditionally, also embraced a child-centred view of the learning process. Topics have been seen as one way to engage the curiosity and creativity of pupils and to encourage them, through discovery, to direct their own learning. This may not sound like National Curriculum rhetoric, but references to investigative, problem-solving learning styles and to collaborative group work can be found liberally scattered through the Orders for the core and other foundation subjects. The whole of the new science Attainment Target 1 is about 'Scientific Investigation'. The whole of the programme of study for design and technology capability at Key Stage 1 can be seen as a problem-solving curriculum. Words like 'explore', 'experience', 'investigate' and 'find out about' are used in the programmes of study for mathematics, science, technology, geography and history. These words suggest that pupils should be active in the learning process, engaging their curiosity and creativity, as well as being passively 'taught' new skills and knowledge. References to collaboration and co-operation between pupils are frequently met with.

The English document (DES, 1989) refers to 'working in groups', 'discussion of work with pupils', 'collaborative play' and 'collaborations with other pupils'. In completing the programme of study for design and technology capability at Key Stage 1, pupils should have experience of 'working in teams' (DES 1990). The orders for Science (DES, 1991d) require pupils to respond to the 'ideas of other pupils and become involved in group activities'. It was clearly the intention of those who defined the details of the National Curriculum that pupils should learn, for a significant proportion of the time, through enquiry and collaboration. It is simply not possible to accept the content of the National Curriculum without also accepting messages about teaching approaches and learning styles. The issues, in National Curriculum documentation, are inextricably linked.

The medium is the message

Before this contention is employed as another weapon in the armoury of the disapplication lobby, it might be prudent to return to a question raised earlier. Do these considerations about teaching approaches and learning styles apply in schools for pupils with learning difficulties where there is already a fierce debate about the relevance of the subject content of the National Curriculum? Why should such schools, with a record of successful intervention through the use of their own tried and tested methodology, adopt a new set of hypotheses?

The non-statutory guidance for mathematics (NCC, 1989) puts the argument for cross-curricular teaching succinctly: 'In life, experiences do not come in separate packages with subject labels'. This statement transcends all the familiar rationalisations, which themselves carry a great deal of persuasive weight, about efficiency and the exploitation of links and overlap. It is not simply saying that teachers can save time and energy by addressing related issues through cross-curricular schemes of work. It suggests that reality for pupils, indeed for any of us, is a complex phenomenon and that learning experiences, if they are to be truly effective, should reflect that complexity. In schools for pupils with severe learning difficulties teachers have devoted many years to the attempt to simplify experience by chopping it up into separate categories (this is cognitive; that is language) and then chopping up the separate categories into isolated skills and subskills and fragments of skills before feeding these fragments of skills to pupils piecemeal and out of context. Disappointment has been expressed because, to paraphrase frequently heard complaints, pupils with learning difficulties 'do not generalise' and 'fail to transfer their skills'. Why is this a surprise? They have not been taught about generalisation and transferability; they have been taught about the separation, isolation and fragmentation of skills. Surely learning is most effective when it takes place in contexts which allow pupils to see the relevance and application of what they are learning; contexts which mirror reality as closely as possible? Hence, reality is cross-curricular and thematically linked and the connections between ideas are often more useful as learning routes than the boundaries which have been imposed upon them.

Arguments can also be advanced to support enquiry, investigation and creative problem solving in the learning process. The pupil's role in the behaviourist view of education is almost entirely passive. The teacher prescribes what, when and how the pupil is to learn. The pupil's task is simply to receive effectively. The National Curriculum, on the other hand, requires pupils to be more active participants in the teacher–learner relationship. Again, teachers in schools for pupils with learning difficulties have a characteristic complaint, focused upon perceived shortcomings in the pupils themselves, which suggests that in spite of years of careful training, pupils somehow lack the self-confidence to go out and put their skills into practice in the real world. It is unlikely however that pupils who have been encouraged throughout their school careers to be the passive recipients of a system of instruction which seeks to eradicate failure and guarantee success, will suddenly become proactive adults brimming with self-esteem, simply because they are confronted with the challenges of the real world. The confidence to ask questions, seek solutions, investigate new situations and experiment with new skills and attitudes grows with experience. Learning opportunities which encourage pupils to develop their ability to enquire, challenge, innovate, recover from error and solve their own problems can be provided in school within the boundaries of a risk-taking policy and in dialogue with an empathic teacher. It will be these experiences which give pupils not only the skills necessary to put on and take off clothes, but also the sense that they have the right to shop for garments which they prefer and the self-confidence to figure out their way home when they become lost in the shopping centre.

In a very similar way the subtle outcomes of group endeavour may often be denied to pupils with learning difficulties by a teaching regime which relies extensively upon the one-to-one teacher–pupil relationship. Again pupils may be described as isolated from their peers, or as lacking social skills when much of their experience at school promotes these very characteristics. The tendency is to emphasise deficits in the pupil instead of inadequacies in the teaching system. This is not to suggest that pupils who are genuinely emotionally vulnerable or socially withdrawn do not exist. But pupils who have rarely had the opportunity to work as a member of a team or to negotiate roles for themselves within a co-operative enterprise will find it difficult to adjust, for instance, to the interpersonal rigours of life in a group home.

The goal of autonomy

Teachers in schools for pupils with severe and moderate learning difficulties often claim that their aim is to educate pupils for autonomy. This is, of course, a worthy aim but autonomy is about more than proficiency in skills. Many people have criticised the narrow, prescriptive nature of the objectives based curriculum. But there is a danger, in proposing alternatives, of constructing something that amounts simply to a prescriptive, objectives based curriculum with a degree of increased breadth.

Attempts to analyse the skills involved in enquiry, problem solving or collaboration may be very helpful but, to an extent, they miss the point. Any reputable mainstream definition of personal and social education will include reference to teaching approaches and learning styles and to the effect, positive or otherwise, which they can have upon the self esteem and self-confidence of pupils.These definitions propose a measured devolution of central control from teachers to pupils – a deliberate policy of power sharing. The issue, viewed from this perspective, is not whether teachers can devise ever more sophisticated sets of skills to teach their pupils under ever more subtle conditions but whether teachers have the courage to support their pupils in taking increasing responsibility for their own learning. The rhetoric claims, after all, that the intention of teachers is to prepare pupils to take control of their own lives. In order to do this pupils require more than just skills. They require the will, the motivation and the determination to put those skills into action. Attributes like these remain resistant to the techniques of skills analysis. They will continue to be fostered only in teacher–pupil interactions which are characterised by genuine dialogue and by a sincere commitment to the task of enabling pupils to become self-actuating. As Paulo Friere (1972) says in *Pedagogy of the Oppressed*; 'Authentic education is not carried on by A *for* B or by A *about* B but rather by A *with* B, mediated by the world.'

Chapter Seven

Taking Control with the Help of the Technical and Vocational Education Initiative and Records of Achievement

Steve Parker

Introduction

It is a sad fact of life that much of the educational legislation imposed on the teaching profession during the past decade has been introduced with limited consultation and at a pace that has tested the patience and fortitude of even the most committed professional. If one examines the experience of the average teacher of young people with disabilities and significant learning difficulties, the picture is still more extreme. Many colleagues have had to cope with the shock of a new accountability culture and most of us are potential victims of 'initiative burnout'. An added underlying concern throughout this period has been the consistent reality that the interests of pupils with special educational needs were rarely considered from the outset and usually only after initiatives were planned and the special education 'lobby' had done its work. Wedell (1988) and Ashdown, Carpenter and Bovair (1991) offer specific and helpful analysis of this background.

Despite, or perhaps more accurately because of, this experience there has developed a sort of 'Blitz' mentality that has tended to bring out the best in us all. Special educators have learned to interpret rather than subvert the legislation in the interests of their pupils and have made the most of what, at times, have appeared to be inauspicious circumstances.

It is a challenging thought to try to imagine what perception pupils and students with learning difficulties have of this situation. It would be an encouragement to us all to learn that they have perceived both a broadening and deepening of their school curriculum experience and that everyone is increasingly concerned to help realise their hopes and aspirations in a sometimes hostile environment.

This chapter will detail two initiatives, one related developmentally to the other, that are producing positive outcomes for young learning disabled people and which have generally been both formative and professionally satisfying for their teachers. It will describe the process by which the Technical and Vocational Education Initiative (TVEI) has developed nationally since its launch in 1983; how Technical and Vocational Education (TVE) is being delivered in the City of Birmingham; and will share the experience of Fox Hollies, a fifty-place secondary school for students with severe learning difficulties (SLD). It will then explore the relationship between TVEI and Records of Achievement (ROA) and their combined effect on the curriculum and organisation of schools, describing the principles and processes of ROA and discussing some of the problems that have been encountered (and in many instances solved) in their delivery for students with special educational needs (SEN).

Throughout this analysis there will be illustrations of the many ways in which both initiatives have benefited and empowered young people with learning difficulties. The aim will be to demonstrate that the ultimate impact has been to raise their expectations. In so doing, however, the author will seek to offer the respectful caveat that we must all, most especially post-school providers, do all that we can to meet those raised expectations.

The Technical and Vocational Education Initiative (TVEI)

The first TVEI pilot projects commenced in 1983 after the Manpower Services Commission invited Local Education Authorities (LEAs) to submit proposals for taking part. Fourteen LEAs, of which Birmingham was one, became involved and by 1987 there were 89 participating authorities in England and Wales.

The purpose of the scheme was to explore and test methods of organising, delivering, managing and resourcing sustainable programmes of general, technical and vocational education for 14 to 18 year olds. Its general objective was to widen and enrich the curriculum in a way that would help young people to prepare for the world of work and to develop skills and interests, including creative abilities, that would help them to lead a fuller life and to be able to contribute more to the life of the community (The Training Agency, 1989a)

The inherent characteristics of the initiative from its outset were flexibility and adaptability in relation to national and local need. It is of interest to note that, during the pilot phase, many LEAs and schools were confused and sometimes discomfited by working within such a model. Research of the pilot phase identified a number of negative issues, perhaps most important of which were:

- the weakness of the cohort principle, whereby TVEI enhancement was limited to a small number of selected (often less able) pupils;
- short planning-time leading to some unfocused work and a waste of resources;
- the title TVEI tending to limit the involvement of many subject specialists and creating confusion and discontinuity in relation to the cross-curricular nature of some of the objectives.

These experiences were, however, extremely formative, and by the time already participating and newly recruited LEAs became involved in the extension phase from 1988 onwards, many lessons had been learned and applied to the formation of future models of delivery. The essential features which have proved to be effective are:

(1) the development of local consortium structures that involve all institutions and staff in TVEI plans which are based on clear LEA policy;
(2) systems of accountability right through to central government that allow individual institutions maximum flexibility in spending their developed budgets;
(3) a consensus view of entitlement for *all* students in a major curriculum development project that was later to prove important in relation to delivery of the emerging National Curriculum;
(4) all plans should work towards the development of teaching styles that give students greater participation in and control of their learning, problem solving, and activities related to the world of work.

Although few special schools were involved in the TVEI pilot schemes (often as an afterthought, particularly in post-16 provision) there were early signs of undoubted curricular benefits for their students. Advantages included a broadening of the curriculum to include a range of experiences not previously available, raised expectations of students and improved resources from working with other institutions. The involvement of special schools, including those for students with severe learning difficulties, became a more prominent feature of the extension phase.

A report from Her Majesty's Inspectorate (DES and Welsh Office, 1991) deals very thoroughly with the first seven years of the TVEI programme, through pilot to the start of the extension phase, and provides valuable insights into the programmes. It highlights successes whilst not ignoring some of the false starts which were made in the early days. It is now fascinating to reflect on the concerns being expressed about TVEI and other contemporary initiatives, regarding their relevance and potential value for young people with special educational needs.

In her editorial introduction to a special issue of the British Journal of Special Education, Margaret Peter (1987) asked '*Whose* Initiatives?' and questioned whether the new national curriculum and training initiatives 'belonged' to those with special education needs or whether 'ownership' was confined largely to the majority of school and college students who do not have significant learning difficulties. In the same issue of the Journal, however, Deborah Cooper (1987) was reminding readers that one of the original stated aims of TVEI was to cater for young people *across the ability range*. She pointed out that although there were a number of examples of students with learning difficulties being included in the pilot, opportunities were not at that stage equalised and it appeared that it was 'those with the most severe and complex difficulties who had least access to the TVEI'. Nonetheless she felt optimistic because under the extension of TVEI, criteria specifically required that students with SEN be included. There is much evidence to support the fact that this was indeed the case over the next four years.

In the introduction to its *TVEI Special Education Needs Directory*, the Training Agency (1986b) reminded readers that Education Authorities were required to develop strategies to ensure that young people with SEN receive an education which provides: a practical and relevant curriculum; competencies, knowledge and appropriate qualifications and accreditation; direct opportunities to experience the world of work through work shadowing or work experience; opportunities for working together, to develop essential personal and interpersonal skills; and enhanced guidance and counselling.

Despite the weight of information in its bulky 557 page format the *Directory* failed to meet its own brief. Whilst containing many examples of the excellent work of those institutions and individuals which sought to deliver these entitlements, the machinery for producing the directory could not keep pace with the extraordinary rate of change taking place in the field, and so never gave a truly accurate picture.

The Midlands TVEI Special Needs Steering Group (1991) has produced four annual digests of interesting practice which focus directly on the wide variety of learning experiences and opportunities supported by TVEI in the region for students with special needs. These digests are typical of the regional newsletters published regularly throughout the country.

A specific example of the involvement of SLD students in the Leicestershire TVEI extension programme is provided by Cassell, Lindoe and Skilling (1991).

Within these publications, along with feedback from meetings, courses and conferences, there is a consistent message that TVEI has contributed significantly towards an enrichment of the curriculum for young people with learning difficulties. Through participation in such diverse opportunities as integration into neighbouring mainstream schools, work-related courses and work experience placement, widening community links, mini-enterprises, attendance on link and full-time FE college courses, involvement in integrated arts programmes, increasingly ambitious residential activities and a generally more reactive and choice-based curriculum, students have noticeably enhanced self esteem and self-advocacy skills.

It is worthy of note that this period in special education has witnessed significant changes in the way that teachers of pupils with learning difficulties have approached their responsibilities as enablers in the learning process. Smith (1991) suggests that over the past decade teachers in special education have increasingly adopted a critically reflective approach to classroom practice and assumed responsibility for their own professional development. As a result there is growing support for a more interactive relationship between the teacher and those taught, in which the learner is an active partner in the process. Elsewhere she (Smith, 1988) and others (Fagg, 1991; Bovair, 1990) have discussed the increasing range of proven and acceptable teaching styles that are leading to a more eclectic and ultimately more effective approach to the education of young people with learning difficulties.

In their professional interactions with colleagues in the mainstream, facilitated and encouraged through the TVEI, teachers in special schools have frequently played a useful and valued role. Their thoughtful and analytical student-centred approach to their work has often sparked much useful and productive debate about learning styles, and the interplay of working practices has served to influence practice on both sides of an increasingly narrowing divide between mainstream and special. This phenomenon has undoubtedly improved the sense of professional competence and self-worth amongst special school teachers and, in the inevitably symbiotic relationship between participants in the learning process, students have been happy to attempt to meet the increasingly ambitious expectations of their teachers.

Note: Since this chapter was written the results of a national research project which studied the impact of TVEI on young people with special educational needs has been published (Employment Department, 1992). The evidence from the study paints a very positive picture and echoes many of the foregoing conclusions.

The Birmingham model

Following its unhappy experiences in the pilot phase, the Birmingham LEA sought, and was granted, an extremely valuable development year (1989/90) by the Training Agency. This enabled full consultation with all interested parties and resulted in a detailed draft submission to the Department of Employment in September 1990.

The City's compact urban character facilitated an almost unique delivery model based on eight self-selected TVEI partnerships which reflect geographical and institutional variety. Most of the partnerships comprise a mix of up to a dozen mainstream secondary schools, a Further Education College and a special school. Others incorporate a greater number of both mainstream and special schools.

The LEA's management strategy allows the partnerships delegated responsibility for spending 85 per cent of the total budget. This devolved budget is operated within a set of agreed principles and a tight framework of monitoring and evaluation. The system therefore offers maximum flexibility whilst requiring maximum accountability, producing a model that has been described as having unity of purpose without uniformity of delivery. Most participating institutions and individuals have appreciated such an approach that has put the focus of control near to the centre of delivery, giving practitioners full responsibility for making the initiative work.

In order to counteract one of the criticisms that was levelled at the pilot phase, an upper limit of 25 per cent of the budget for spending on capital equipment was imposed. As a consequence the vast proportion of expenditure has been invested in people. Each project has a full-time coordinator supported by a staff team, the character of which is determined by the partnership's Management Group, which in the main comprises the head teachers and principals of the member institutions. The majority of staffing costs have provided cover and out-of-hours payments for teachers to work within school and on a cross-institutional basis, to develop and deliver the range of curriculum opportunities described in a support document, *The TVE Entitlements* (Birmingham City Council, 1990). The LEA's approach to curriculum entitlement can be summarised thus:

Key principles

- Equal opportunities
- Continuity and progression
- Broad, balanced curriculum
- Community partnership

Themes and processes

- Progressive work-related activity
- Student-centred learning and formative assessment
- Problem-solving technological activities in all areas of the curriculum
- Enterprise education as part of economic awareness
- Careers education and guidance

Common learning outcomes

- Appropriate nationally recognised qualifications and a Post 16 Record of Achievement. (ROA)

Included under this heading would be a range of skills including: effective communications, aesthetic sensitivity and creativity, effective personal and interpersonal skills, the capacity to work independently and in teams, the ability to cope positively with change and the capacity to solve problems and formulate action plans. In addition students should have opportunities to engage in a range of physical activities to promote physical development and to develop an understanding of the importance of a healthy lifestyle.

Staff from special schools have worked collaboratively within their host partnerships and have often been pleased to recognise that much of the underlying philosophy subsumed in these entitlements is already incorporated in their own schools' curriculum. Involvement with TVE has, however, made teachers very aware of the frequent disparity between entitlement and access. It has encouraged us to consciously seek a widening of practical and experiential approaches, and students have been the beneficiaries. The later section on Records of Achievement will examine the ways in which we have come to credit students who have learning difficulties with the capabilities of independent thinking, decision making and taking responsibility for their own excellence. These young people have consistently repaid that respect with their achievements.

The Fox Hollies experience

Fox Hollies entered TVEI in its first year of extension as a phase 1 school of the South Eastern Partnership, which incorporates the local FE College (which provides an administrative base for the Partnership Coordinator and his staff) and eight mainstream secondary schools.

From the outset it was recognised that as a small school with a teaching establishment of Head, Deputy and six classroom teachers it would be very stretched if it were to play its full part in the partnership. The school made an early decision that overall management of TVE should be shared jointly between the Head and Deputy and that the Deputy Head should represent it, in both the Partnership Management and Executive Groups. The senior management then set about engineering a whole school approach to TVE delivery involving all staff, teachers and Special Schools Assistants (SSAs) alike. The Partnership has a number of development and planning Task Groups and the school had teacher representatives on as many as it considered appropriate and viable. There were in-school 'Shadow' Task Groups doing development work on priority curriculum areas. (At the time of writing these are careers education and guidance, assessment and recording, including ROA and 16+ continuity and progression; earlier groups focused on work related education and science and technology.) The funding has allowed for an extra teacher to be employed one day a week throughout the year to cover teachers involved in development work or INSET. This has proved an invaluable resource and has facilitated productive work with the Curriculum Development Tutors (CDTs), a unique partnership resource. The CDTs were recruited early in the life of the Partnership to cover such areas as the core curriculum, equal opportunities, ROA, information technology and science. Working closely with staff in all the member institutions they have been crucial in all of the school's development work and to the success of TVE in the Partnership. The Head and Deputy were involved in the CDTs appointments and it is evident that the work that they have done in Fox Hollies has been of professional benefit to all.

It is difficult to disentangle those developments at Fox Hollies that are a direct result of its involvement with TVE; but this is perhaps a measure of how embedded the entitlements have become. It can, however, be said that there is no likelihood of the Hawthorne Effect applying (Cohen and Bradley, 1978) and that there have been many lasting tangible benefits for the school's students.

At the core of the changes has been the development of a thematic model of curriculum delivery, incorporating nine termly themes over a three-year period. Theme titles include, for example, Sight and Sound, Our World, Family and Family Life, and have been chosen to cover the widest possible spread of National Curriculum subjects, whilst embracing important cross-curricular themes and entitlements. The structure has been designed to deliver themes age-appropriately, offering staged progression when themes are revisited. It is possible to incorporate Individual Teaching Programmes (ITPs) into the planning process and, of course, to differentiate delivery according to student need. Students with profound and multiple learning difficulties experience the full range of curricular experience alongside their more able peers, with obvious and positive outcomes for all students.

As a corollary to this, approximately a third of the school's population in years nine to 11 have been involved in a number of integrated technology projects with students of the same age from a Partnership school. Working alternately in both settings (workshop facilities in the mainstream school proving to be of major value to Fox Hollies' students), the carefully structured projects have been of positive and mutual benefit, engendering understanding and reciprocal respect for both groups (Moseley School, 1991). It is to be hoped that some of that benefit could apply in the longer term as both sets of students move on to further education and out into the wider community as young adults (Carpenter and Lewis, 1989).

Whilst accepting that the majority of students at Fox Hollies will probably never be given the opportunity to have paid, open employment, the school nonetheless expects that many of them will find themselves in work-type situations. It is certainly accepted that they have underlying educational entitlement to learn about the world of work and to understand the workings of industry and commerce through work related activities. From an early stage all students are encouraged to take responsibility for specific tasks within school, first of all within the classroom and later in the wider school community. For example, the job of collecting, photocopying and then distributing information for the Daily News Sheet is given to students; many similar jobs are shared on a rota basis. When students move into the Further Education Unit at age 16 they become involved with more sophisticated activities like mini enterprises and ultimately go on work experience placements. The range of placements, which started originally within the local community centre – where students help in the playgroup, serve meals in the old people's luncheon club, look after the animals and tend the garden in the environment centre – is rapidly expanding to offer a wider choice. Many of the out-of-school opportunities for visits and work experience placements have been as a result of the school's involvement with Industrial Tutors and Compact.

Compact is a direct partnership of employers, schools/colleges, students and their parents, where each makes a commitment to help increase the awareness and access of young people to worthwhile training and jobs (Training Agency, 1989c). Three Compact Tutors are currently working with a cohort of seven Fox Hollies students on student Compact goals, especially adapted to take account of their circumstances. The standard goals require students to complete coursework satisfactorily and on time, to achieve a high standard of attendance and punctuality, to develop personal skills and qualities and to take part in work related activities. It has been of particular benefit to involve parents in this exercise. They have been enormously creative in helping to adapt the goals and happy to cooperate in enabling and supporting their children to meet those goals. In some ways staff view this initiative as being probably one of the most productive for their students. Involving, as it does, professionals from outside the education system it has the potential to consolidate the earlier years of home/school work and create a new shared venture (Wolfendale, 1989), relating to the young people's lives beyond school.

A modular structure for the 16+ years curriculum, giving students options and control over their learning choices, is gradually being developed in the school. Many of the elements already mentioned are incorporated and mini enterprise and arts projects are important additions. The Badgers Badge Making Company has been established in the school for over two years, functioning as an autonomous operation with its own management group and bank account. It has fulfilled many large orders and made impressive profits which have either been ploughed back into the business or used to fund other initiatives, especially arts projects. Other mini enterprises, which include manufacturing jewellery or making sandwiches and hot snacks as alternative staff lunches, have also been profitable and have supported other activities (in one instance an educational trip to France).

TVE sponsored Creative Arts initiatives have involved students in workshops with an Asian dance artist and drummer and with a musician who enabled them to create their own electronic music composition. Both workshops have led to performances in Partnership Arts Projects, working with and alongside mainstream peers. Students not directly involved in the workshops have benefited through being an audience to presentations and also by working in drama activities using the music produced as a stimulus.

Galletley (1989) has suggested that the aims of such a new curriculum are to make young people more employable (or more productively unemployed) and to demonstrate to them the significant connection between what we are like and what we achieve. Planning within the school has worked to this end, with the hope that by presenting students with the right opportunities they will be helped to develop the appropriate attributes which will give them greater confidence and self esteem, independence of mind and action and self advocacy skills. The Records of Achievement process, which should ultimately be at the centre of this self-actualisation, is the last of those developments that TVE has helped the school to establish.

The leavers-group teacher has met with the many post school providers, including those FE Colleges who offer link and full time courses to students, to consult with them and share the school's aspirations for its students. The school's curriculum content and delivery has been compared with theirs and attempts made to share curriculum development, where appropriate, to enable the students' successful transition.

Records of Achievement

The history of ROAs is a long and sometimes confusing saga, but it is important to recognise that as long ago as the mid 1940s, a clearly stated concern for the needs of the less able school leaver to have some form of meaningful 'leaving document' set the debate in motion. The thinking was that, while external exams provided motivation and reward for the more able pupils, those of average ability and below gained nothing from them but reminders of inadequacy and failure.

It took some forty years of debate and individual initiatives to provide school leavers with a statement of their achievement, both within and across the curriculum, before the DES issued a policy statement in 1984.

There were also some attempts to recognise activities outside the school setting as being germane to providing a true picture of the individual pupil. The stated policy was to have ROAs in place in the secondary sector by 1990, and to this end nine education support grant-funded pilot schemes were set up covering 22 authorities and 250 schools. The schemes were required to report annually to the newly established Records of Achievement Steering Committee (RANSC) which was aided in its deliberations by the Pilot Records of Achievement in Schools Evaluation (PRAISE).

Although the pilots provided a variety of conclusions, there was a clear consensus of opinion that remains intact through subsequent contention, and forms the basis of most schemes. ROAs are seen as having both formative and summative functions. The formative *process* of profiling is, ideally, ongoing throughout the pupil's school career and, if properly managed can be both motivating and constructive. As it relates to fully integrated recording and assessment systems it should provide opportunities for a continuing dialogue between the student and teacher, involving parents wherever appropriate. It should recognise, acknowledge and give credit for what the student has achieved and experienced in the widest possible terms both in and out of school. It should also be diagnostic, in so much as that it evaluates the effectiveness of curriculum organisation and teaching, analysing the strengths and weaknesses of the work of students.

The summative record is the final leaving document which gives a rounded portrayal of the student, emphasising positive achievements and incorporating evidence in its widest sense. Central to the ROA philosophy is the notion that the summative document and all the supporting portfolio of evidence is owned by the student.

It does not profit us to detail here the tortuous trail of events that led to the launch of the National Record of Achievement (NRA) in early 1991. Much of the story is told lucidly by Broadfoot *et al.* (1991) and readers will need to update themselves on the latest policy.

However, despite continued uncertainties, each change seems to give some new impetus to ROAs in schools, and teachers and those taught continue to recognise the value of the ROA concept. What is important in the context of this chapter is that, in this uncertain policy environment, TVEI extension carried forward the ROA banner. Not only did TVEI provide the appropriate resources to support the necessary changes to teaching and learning that ROAs required, but the Training Agency made it a condition for all schools entering TVEI at the extension phase to provide ROAs for their students. At that time, in the absence of a positive government response to the RANSC recommendations, many LEAs, Birmingham included, set out to explore ways of putting principle into practice. The outcome has been a range of localised models with many similarities, which will probably have to be amended to meet the finalised requirements of the NRA for students completing compulsory education in 1993.

Special schools have been involved from the outset and many of the ROA principles, for example criterion referenced diagnostic assessment leading to the development of individualised learning programmes, were already embedded in their working practices. More problematic, particularly for students with learning difficulties, has been the question of self assessment and individual student reviews. Most of us are still at the experimental stage, using a range of materials, including photography, video, audio tape, Rhebus and Makaton symbols and computer software to prompt and focus students' thoughts. A number of authors have shared their approaches to these problems, notably Cassell, Lindoe and Skilling (1991), Conquest, Pirt and Wright (1990), The London Record of Achievement (1989) and contributors to the West Midlands Monitoring Group SLD *Broadcast No 5: Assessment* (1991). What has become increasingly plain is that we can only develop those finely-tuned tutor review skills which are a necessary focus to work in this way by using those facilities of active listening, open-ended questioning and enthusiasm that we already utilise in our day-to-day teaching. We need to openly share our experiences both within and beyond school (always respecting the specific confidences that we have shared with the students) in order to better understand the challenge that we face.

In the meantime, the staff at Fox Hollies know that their experience in relation to defining the concept of achievement is not uncommon. From the earliest stage of their ROA planning they realised that they had to be clear about what constituted excellence for each student, that a curriculum must be provided that created opportunities for this success and, perhaps most important for everyone involved, that such success was recognised and celebrated publicly. Their own approach to these challenges has been to create an ethos of positive practice which enables each student to set their own agenda, to develop the curriculum that has already been described and to construct a system of merit badges that relates to the student's particular type of achievement (work, social or community). Everyone can then share that success at the daily assembly, with students explaining their own achievements wherever possible. The award is then recorded on personal profiles.

ROAs are already proving very effective in helping students to understand their own needs and empowering them to negotiate their own learning. By providing sensitive ongoing support, encouragement and guidance the approach enables them to see their own learning in the wider context of the society of which they are increasingly becoming valued members.

[**Author's acknowledgments** I would like to thank Kathryn O'Leary (who as Deputy Head Teacher at Fox Hollies had a significant influence on all our work, most particularly in relation to TVE) for her support and encouragement in the writing of this chapter. I would also wish to thank colleagues, both at school and in the LEA, who have contributed in many ways. Special thanks must go to the students who constantly inspire us all.]

Chapter Eight

The Role of a Student Committee in Promotion of Independence among School Leavers

Keith Winup

'And does he take sugar?'

Normalisation, the principle put forward by Wolfensberger (1972), starts from the premise that a major handicap of people with learning difficulties is their devaluation in society. In order to remedy this, they need as far as possible to have experiences that are generally valued in society and to achieve a valued status. Williams and Shoultz (1982) state that an integral part of normalisation is that people with learning difficulties have a say in their lives and should be given the opportunity to learn useful and self enhancing skills.

A fundamental aim of teaching older pupils, as Hewlett (1986) illustrates, is the promotion of social and personal skills and preparation for adult life. Pupils with learning difficulties are no exception to this principle. However there are barriers to achieving adult status for this population as they do not often present a positive self image. This can create stigma in the eyes of society and restrict the degree of participation and interaction. It is therefore a priority for schools to find ways of promoting independence and self-assertion for pupils with learning difficulties.

People's behaviour tends to be profoundly affected by the role expectations that are placed upon them and they generally play the roles they have been assigned. Wolfensberger (1972) points out the labels, concepts, stereotypes, role perceptions and expectancies applied to persons with learning difficulties which affect their self concept and the ways in which they are likely to respond. Hence, it is important to break down negative attitudes and to encourage our pupils to develop a richer and more adult relationship with their environment.

The area of self-advocacy has an important role to play in developing and generalising these skills in preparation for dealing with the real world. Self-advocacy highlights the importance of offering choices, providing opportunities for decision making and for effecting change. Self-advocacy is not just another curricular subject, to be taught once a week; it must affect each day's activities and permeate throughout all areas of the curriculum. It is identified as a cross-curricular theme in *Education for Citizenship*: 'Elements of it can and must be taught through the subjects of the National Curriculum and other timetabled provision, enriched and reinforced by being woven into the wider work of the school' (NCC, 1990).

Extra curricular activities, such as the formation of a student committee, are also important in providing opportunities to enhance skills, exercise responsibility and apply knowledge and understanding gained through work carried out in the classroom. Figure 8.2 highlights the aspects which form part of the curriculum of post 16 students with learning difficulties which relate to self-advocacy and which will be reinforced in the course of participation in a student committee.

Why a student committee?

A priority in working within a post 16 department of a school for pupils with learning difficulties is to create learning situations and environments which assist in promoting and achieving more independence for individual pupils. The curriculum for pupils with learning difficulties, particularly for post 16 students, must encourage pupils to become more independent, to make more choices and exert more control over their environment.

Our post 16 department is situated in a separate building from the main school and puts these principles into action by creating a more adult environment than that in the main school. There are different expectations of students and an increasing degree of personal independence and responsibility. The students have their own common room for which they are responsible and are also required to make decisions on a variety of options in the timetable. These include having a voice in leisure module pursuits, work experience placements within and outside school, and world-of-work module activities.

It was from within this framework that it seemed a logical, although challenging, step to set up a student committee. A committee appeared to be an appropriate vehicle in which self-advocacy could have practical application.

The committee was seen as an opportunity to encourage students to voice their opinions, by providing a channel to express ideas, initiatives and feelings regarding the place in which they spend a large proportion of their time. As Flynn (1991) and Wolfensberger (1972) suggest, people with learning difficulties are in a weak position to speak up for themselves and therefore need opportunities on the timetable for training and experience. However, the problem is not only about encouraging pupils to have a voice but also involves creating an environment in which there is a partnership between the students and those that work with them. Establishing a committee was seen as a step in this direction.

Establishing a committee for post 16 students is an appropriate age related activity. It is an operation which provides training and experience in making decisions along with fellow peers and also one in which emerging adult status can be recognised. It assists in the process by which people confront their own situation, coming to some understanding of it and developing some control over it (Dumbleton, 1990).

Ideas into action

Two class groups comprising 22 students with learning difficulties, ranging from severe to moderate, were involved. After the decision to establish the committee, several sessions under the curriculum area of citizenship were used to explore the related issues. Trial elections were held to familiarise the students with the election process and particular emphasis was directed to establishing the need for certain qualities for particular jobs. It was found that some students were voting for the person and not the required qualities of character, even when the person (teacher in role) had presented negative qualities for a particular job. It was evident that more work was necessary in order to highlight the significance of key qualities and key words. Subsequent sessions involved looking at key words relevant to qualities pertinent to committee members. The following were highlighted as key words:

friendly	good worker	talks up	distractable
helpful	lazy	quiet	reliable
unhelpful	honest	good listener	imaginative

Various sessions using role play and discussion were used to explore these qualities to increase understanding and significance. The role of a committee was also investigated and student contributions revealed the following concepts:

- working together;
- arranging activities and clubs;

- improving the student common room;
- helping students with problems;
- arranging trips and visits;
- raising money;
- deciding what action to take about silly people;
- helping decide what should take place during festivals;
- regular weekly meetings.

Students forwarded 14 nominations for the committee and over the course of several weeks these candidates prepared, with the aid of staff, individual manifestos relevant to their personal qualities. Videos were made of the candidates presenting their manifestos and they were encouraged to express the reasons why they should be selected, in front of the group. The election day was arranged and publicised, with further work on the process of voting using a ballot sheet. The ballot sheets had photocopied pictures of the candidates to make identification easier. The elections proved stimulating and six students were elected. The whole process was recorded on video to use as an aid in further reflection on the election process.

The selection of the committee resulted in an equal representation of the sexes and of severe and moderate learning difficulties, which provided an interesting balance. Voters had considered qualities of the candidates and had voted in favour of students who had definite and caring characters and who spoke up for themselves. It was interesting that a large percentage of students did not just vote for close friends, and two students who exert control and influence by force in the common room were discriminated against by a complete lack of votes. The student voting had demonstrated democratic potential! The profile of committee members is shown in Figure 8.1.

	Sex	Age	Learning difficulty	Personality
MEMBER 1	M	16	Severe	Distractable, isolated, talks up, determined, socially timid, self-sufficient.
MEMBER 2	F	16	Moderate	Insecure, sensitive, self-critical, lacks confidence, responsible, caring.
MEMBER 3	M	18	Moderate	Tough, unsure of self, has mind of own, influenced by others.
MEMBER 4	F	18	Severe	Assertive, courageous, confident, caring.
MEMBER 5	M	17	Severe	Self-orientated, petulant, attention seeking, speaks up, assertive, has ideas of his own, a loner.
MEMBER 6	F	17	Moderate	Extrovert, gregarious, likes to be centre of attention, intolerant.

Figure 8.1: Profile of elected committee members

The diversity of qualities and needs of the committee members provided a range of examples of how each individual could develop self-advocacy skills, through involvement within the committee. The specific needs of individuals on the committee relate to various areas within self-advocacy, in particular the areas of decision making, speaking up for oneself, relating and expressing oneself to others and solving problems (see Figure 8.2). The group dynamics within a committee can foster skills that need to be developed at various levels for all members.

	Qualities to offer	**Individual Needs**
MEMBER 1	Good vocabulary, keen to help, motivated, keen interest in world around him.	Improved attention span and listening skills, relating comments to issue, speaking more slowly, improving inter-active skills, listening to another's point of view, problem solving.
MEMBER 2	Reliable, takes the initiative, shows concern for others, co-operative.	Extending vocabulary and experiences, problem solving, expressing own ideas developing confidence, speaking up in front of others. Needs to be in a small group.
MEMBER 3	Anxious to help, considerate tolerant, friendly, speaks up, interacts with others.	Expressing ideas, thinking things through, listening to others' points of view, problem solving.
MEMBER 4	Friendly, tolerant, co-operative caring.	Extending vocabulary, listening to others, problem solving, expressing ideas, considering alternatives to a problem, working as part of a group.
MEMBER 5	Reliable, good concentration lots of ideas, perseverance.	Improving articulation, repeating words in order to be understood by others, developing confidence, accepting new ideas, listening to others' points of view, speaking in front of others.

108

| MEMBER 6 | Lively, popular, artistic, lots of ideas, literate. | Improving listening and understanding skills, problem solving, becoming more receptive to others' points of view, seeing a task through from start to completion, working without distraction. |

Figure 8.2: Qualities and needs of individual committee members

Development of the committee

Early sessions involved exploring the running of a committee and the election and role of officers.

The role of chairperson was discussed and defined as:
● to open a meeting;
● to make sure that each member who wants to speak is given an opportunity to do so;
● to make sure one person speaks at a time;
● to keep members to the point being discussed;
● to make a decision by calling a vote;
● to end the meeting.

The role of the secretary was defined as:
● to write the agenda for meetings;
● to write up the minutes;
● to recall the minutes at each meeting. (The minutes could be taped and typed out on a computer.)

The role of the treasurer was defined as:
● to keep account of all monies;
● to open and look after a bank account.

A member of staff acted in the role of advisor to the committee in order to introduce and teach the above skills during meetings and at other appropriate times during the timetable.

The role of the advisor was defined as:
● to become a guide at meetings and not a leader;
● to give assistance and advice when the group needs it;
● to teach the skills of the offices and committee procedure;
● to encourage ideas of the committee which could lead into action.

The committee was in office for a school year and met once a week during the lunch break for at least 20 minutes. Towards the end of the year students from the classes involved in establishing the committee were questioned to investigate their knowledge of its function. Over half the students could name all the committee members and only one student was unable to name any. Although most of the students stated they would go to the committee if they had a problem, very few of them had actually done so. Those who had approached members had complained about students who monopolised the snooker table and computers at lunch time. Such grievances were discussed by the committee and a group solution had to be found in order to address the issue. Ideas were suggested and put into operation in order to observe the outcomes. The eventual solution was a rota of names of students who wanted to use the equipment, giving the times when individuals could use it. This provided a constructive problem solving situation for group discussion, the opportunity to put ideas to the test, to review the situation and establish the solution. All students who wanted to be involved with the activity were able to contribute.

Students were also able to give examples of what the committee had achieved since its formation which included:

- introduction of lunch time activities;
- rotas for the snooker table and computers;
- sponsored events held to raise money;
- new equipment bought from fund raising events (for the common room);
- opening and running of the tuck shop.

At the beginning of the autumn term, when the life of the first committee had ended, several students were asking when the next election would take place. Several were waiting for the return of the committee in order to establish the rota for use of the equipment. The majority of students expressed eagerness to be on the committee and some achieved their aim of being nominated by others. In the second year of the committee only one of the past members was re-elected.

Areas promoted by a student committee

Some of the areas that are promoted during the development of a student committee are briefly reviewed below.

Continuity

The establishment of a committee should not occur in isolation, it must be embedded in a whole-school approach to the area of self-advocacy and spill over into classroom work. Although self-advocacy skills are encouraged through the use of a committee, this only affects a small minority of students, who have direct involvement. It is therefore important that the skills of self-advocacy are reinforced and used in the whole timetable for all students. The range of decision making opportunities and areas for self determination within a school timetable is immense and this implies that everyone can take part in self-advocacy at some level, regardless of the severity of their handicap (Wertheimer, 1989).

During the project described above, specific aspects of the role and function of a committee were explained and explored in areas of citizenship; listening to different points of view, and making decisions. Engagement in the voting process was encouraged in a variety of teaching situations. Classroom management, particularly for post 16 pupils, should promote discussion and negotiation regarding the achievement of specific aims and objectives; such an approach is particularly pertinent to the development of Records of Achievement. A method of learning which empowers students to be partners in the learning process encourages them to negotiate constructively and realistically.

Much of the literature on aspects of self-advocacy tends to be concerned with post-school situations but the introduction of advocacy must begin as early as possible in order to develop greater involvement in areas such as decision making. The process should not start within the leavers' programme. If certain skills are taught and developed at earlier stages the greater the prospect for developing independence, assertiveness and responsibility. Interaction between staff throughout the whole school is important in order to discuss relevant issues and become aware of the stages and processes involved in pupils achieving a voice of their own. It is important to develop links with the situations which students will move to on leaving school. They may become eligible candidates to represent other people with learning difficulties at colleges, day centres or residences.

Whelan and Speake (1981) examine self-advocacy in the transition from school to work and identify the knowledge, attitudes and abilities which are important prerequisites for employment. Interaction within the community is an important aspect and Whelan suggests that a person with learning difficulties often seems to exert little influence on his environment whilst it has considerable effect on him. It is within the school environment that initial work can assist in altering this situation.

A working definition of self-advocacy taken from Clare (1990) and Williams and Shoultz (1982) is a useful guide for schools in relation to the aims of a committee. It includes the ability:

- to know what goals and objectives are possible for individuals;
- to choose between goals;

- to express choices, thoughts and feelings with assertiveness if necessary;
- to act upon one's choices to achieve individual objectives;
- to make changes;
- to find help when necessary to achieve specific objectives.

Decision making

Encouraging pupils with learning difficulties to make decisions for themselves is a vital part of the normalisation programme. The use of a student committee provides a valuable vehicle to use decision making skills. Williams and Shoultz (1982) suggest that having the opportunity to make decisions is even more important than the 'rightness' or 'wrongness' of those decisions.

The type of decision making opportunity will obviously depend upon the ability of individuals at a particular time. It was important for the advisor in this project to give support during the early stages of the committee so that members achieved success with decisions and developed confidence and self awareness. The advisor must be sensitive to the needs of individual members, supporting those who need direction and knowing when to stand back to allow particular members to take more control.

Students with severe learning difficulties may experience stress when presented with an apparently simple decision making opportunity, either because they do not have the necessary skills or they are unaware of their right to make a decision in a given situation. This is not surprising 'if you have spent much of your life in a setting which may not have allowed you even to choose whether you want sugar in your tea'. (Whittaker, 1988). A major role of the advisor is to ensure that members speak to the previous speaker and not to the advisor. In the early sessions the advisor was at the hub of the wheel with respect to questions and answers. In later sessions, in order to break down this reliance, pictures were prepared relating to issues on the agenda. The idea was to provide a visual stimulus to assist in the development of individual ideas, decisions and interaction between members.

The ability to make choices is fundamental to becoming self reliant. Programs are therefore necessary throughout schooling to introduce choices of increasing complexity. Through programming, the range of solutions to a particular problem can be explored. During the early stages of the committee the more vocal students, with extrovert characters, tended to take control and quieter students tended to take a back seat role. If the less confident members were consulted they tended to seize upon the solution offered by others. The advisor would often encourage members to make their own contribution and make it clear that when someone was unable to choose it was better to review the issue and provide another opportunity for choice. Boulton (1988) suggests there are a variety of factors which will affect choices made. The knowledge and experiences of the individual will obviously affect the range of possibilities considered when making a decision. How important it is for our pupils to be given experiences in order to increase the basis on which they can make choices.

Participation in a committee offers the opportunity to explore and experience choices. During the discussion of fund raising, some students found it difficult to come up with ideas. Suggestions from their peer group and ideas from the advisor added to their knowledge, and experience was gained as ideas were put into practice. Initial decisions were based on concrete options but members were led towards making choices and decisions by means of less prompting and more open ended questioning.

It is important for post 16 students to take responsibility for decisions once they have been made and to see the consequences. As teachers we should not be over protective and students should be allowed to make mistakes. Learning to cope with a mistake is an essential element of the right to decide for yourself (Wolfensberger, 1972). Wolfensberger also reminds us how everyday life is constantly putting us in situations where we have to take risks and it is through such experiences that we learn to deal with incidents that arise. It is common for people with severe learning difficulties to have people speaking for them and protecting them from the stresses of life. However, if given the opportunity to acquire the appropriate skills many students can become more self reliant. Within the committee, ideas suggested by students were tested when dealing with the snooker table allocation or the question of stolen tapes, for example; various ideas were tested and the most suitable and successful were instigated. These were opportunities to learn by trial and error, to learn from mistakes and to achieve a successful solution.

The need for students to be given time to make decisions is paramount. How often do situations arise where pupils have been rushed or a decision made for them due to the time factor? Similarly, for students to develop decision making skills requires that other people listen and hear. It is important for staff to listen to students' ideas and feelings and to show them that their views are respected and taken into consideration. It is very easy to pay lip service to the principle of decision making without enabling students to develop useful strategies. A committee enables students to develop self-advocacy skills but all to no avail if obstacles are met by negative attitudes from those in control and they are unable to put their ideas into action.

Partnerships

Problems occasionally encountered by the committee were connected with the difficulty that certain staff had in relinquishing aspects of power. Brandon (1988) refers to the question of changes in attitude required for self-advocacy to grow. If attitude problems still exist with professionals then the task of changing attitudes of society at large is an even greater issue. It is important to reflect that it is only by changes in attitude that the place of the handicapped person in society can be improved.

Since most people with learning difficulties are strongly influenced and controlled by parents and professionals, any change towards self-advocacy means challenging traditional ways of thinking and altering the balance of power. The significance of this, as Johnstone (1988) and Wertheimer (1989) point out, is the need for collaborative interaction in this area between parents and other professionals involved with the student.

Both staff and parents must be aware of initiatives and development within the school and be working in partnership with students. Encouraging students to express their own viewpoints will undoubtedly raise concerns about how these might be expressed. It is important that students are aware of the ground rules, understand the diplomacy involved in expressing oneself and that self-advocacy is not an open opportunity to disregard other people's feelings and rights. 'No' has to be said at times and this should be accepted, explained and acted upon when used.

Allowing students to express their feelings and opinions is a necessary preparation for their life post school. The post 16 situation is a time during which important decisions have to be made in terms of post school options, work experience and the beginnings of adult life. Decisions should be firmly based on home–school liaison and a partnership built in the early stage of schooling. Self-advocacy skills cannot just be developed in school; they need to be experienced in the home situation. It is only through consistent commitment of staff and parents to self-advocacy that the individual will develop further independence.

The concept of partnership is also relevant to students in the post 16 department who have profound learning difficulties. Initially, in the role of a citizen advocate, a member of staff represented their interests on the committee. Now that the committee is surmounting its initial problems and members are beginning to assert themselves, it will be important to extend their awareness of others who need to be represented. It is important that ideas for change represent the views of all students, not just those who have a voice to speak out.

Self image

Self image is another important aspect of self-advocacy and an underlying factor in the concept of independence. The aim should be, according to Williams and Shoultz (1982), to give each person a set of beliefs about himself that will engender self confidence, motivation and direction in everyday life. Williams and Shoultz list aspects which need developing within the individual.

(1) I am a unique individual who has a value and worth that is as great as that of anyone else.
(2) Being different does not mean being less valuable.
(3) Everyone has capabilities and limitations.
(4) People should not be judged on their capabilities or limitations but rather on the extent to which they have tried to use their capabilities and overcome their limitations.

It is important that these values are taught to students with learning difficulties, for it is by their adoption that the place of handicapped people in society can be improved. The life experiences of Joseph Deacon (1974) are testimony to the value that should be given to individuals, no matter how handicapped.

The self image of committee members was boosted as they gained a sense of achievement from visible results, not just for themselves but for others. The committee achieved success in establishing lunchtime activities, found solutions for specific problems and for the first time functioned as members of a group. Success in achieving specific goals created a positive attitude and gained respect from other students, staff and parents.

Use of the committee allowed negotiation regarding specific aims and the opportunity to see ideas move from conception into actual production. Initially, the advisor found it necessary to encourage the committee to choose realistic and obtainable goals. The issues dealt with were worked on step by step, with the advisor controlling the initial momentum and reminding the members to keep on target.

Projects involving fund raising opened up larger issues, which took longer to organise but provided the committee with a wider range of learning situations and experiences. The first fund raising project was the idea of a particular member who lacked confidence in herself. The completed sponsored walk provided an unparalleled experience for this student, who saw her ideas put into action and achieving credibility. Such fund raising events involved the introduction and use of a wide range of skills including:

● organisational skills;
● contacting outside agencies for use of an area for walk;

- contacting internal agencies to decide on dates/times;
- relaying information to other students/staff/parents;
- leaflet and poster making;
- planning and marking a route;
- budgeting for and preparing refreshments;
- finding sponsors;
- collecting money and banking it.

The process involved negotiation in order to divide work between members, to take on particular responsibilities and to use people's skills. The advisor and staff were available to be consulted about resources and assistance at each stage. However, the aim was for students to consult staff for assistance and not for staff to take control. It was important for the advisor to make members feel that they all had roles to perform and to channel and use their enthusiasm in a constructive manner. This particular project involved all the students in the post 16 department and raised over £200. It was a significant achievement for the committee and following this they had the task of buying appropriate equipment for the common room. This was carried out by consulting other students for ideas regarding equipment to be purchased. It also required practical number work and budgeting in a way that had never been tried before. Armed with a calculator various stores were visited and eventually purchases were made. The whole exercise was rich in a variety of experiences and learning situations and the end product provided all members with a sense of achievement. The committee is now tackling a jumble sale as a fund raising event.

Conclusion

The use of a student committee is a productive method of developing and experiencing self-advocacy and in particular the promotion of independence, which is paramount for school leavers in their preparation for adult life. A key aspect of transition to adulthood is the establishment of a sense of identity. Most people find support in a peer group who are facing similar challenges; the members of the committee assisted one another in this way. It will be important to eventually extend the work outside the school and develop contact with other committees and learn from their experiences. However, as Lindsay and Marlen (1989) remind us, we must be realistic about such initiatives as they still meet the barriers of old attitudes; there is a danger that by encouraging self-advocacy we may be arousing expectations which cannot be met. There is a need for parents, students and professionals to explore a framework for adulthood for people with learning difficulties. When adults with learning difficulties express their rights to self-determination in public and in action and thus gain and experience respect as citizens, they have something to teach not only to other obviously more capable minority groups, but also to society in general. This says something about the importance of democratic opportunities, the respect due to everyone in a democratic society and that, otherwise, democracy is not complete (Wolfensberger, 1972).

Chapter Nine

Increasing the Personal Effectiveness of Adults in the Community

Huw John and Barbara Speake

When we begin to discuss the personal effectiveness skills of adults with learning disabilities and enabling individuals to take more control over their lives, it is helpful if we think of this as a two-fold process:

- that of helping individuals to acquire skills that are necessary to be more effective; and
- providing opportunities for such skills to be used.

In promoting the philosophy of ordinary living (O'Brien and Tyne, 1981), many authorities responsible for providing services have made attempts to do just this. Model service documents such as that produced by the North Western Regional Health Authority (1982) have outlined steps to be taken to enhance quality of life, to help individuals to exercise choice and to increase competence. Yet the philosophy and the reality do not necessarily always run in parallel as we will see later in this chapter when we discuss some of the dilemmas inherent in helping individuals to take control over their lives.

One of the assumed features characteristic of community care as opposed to institutional care is the opportunities the former provides to enable individuals to take control. Cattermole *et al.* (1988) sought the views of individuals living in a hospital setting about life in the hospital and asked whether or not the individuals wanted to be resettled. Every individual in the study 'wanted to live in the community'. Also of interest were the aspects of their lives in hospital over which they expressed dissatisfaction. One of the main complaints of the 19 individuals surveyed was that of privacy, or the lack of it. Reference was made to: the sharing of rooms; having little opportunity for spending any time alone, little opportunity for peace and quiet; the lack of privacy in bathing (having other residents and/or staff present); having to adhere to strict routines for mealtimes, for getting up and going to bed; the indignity of being counted by staff before going to bed; the stigma that the residents felt about being in the hospital; restrictions on social contacts and authoritarian attitudes of some staff. All these complaints have the same underlying theme – that of control, that of having one's life controlled by others as opposed to being able to control it one's self.

But we may be lulled into a false sense of security if we think that the practices which Cattermole *et al.* (1988) outlined belong only to institutions and to times past. Their study was completed in the mid 1980s and whilst there have been significant numbers of individuals resettled since then, it is still possible to find institutional practices continuing even in community settings. The authors of the above study suggest that planners of services need to take into account the views of individuals with learning disabilities in understanding better how their needs might be met. As these authors say:

> Unfortunately, when mistakes are made in the development of residential services, it is people with mental handicaps who have to live with them, rather than those responsible for the errors. (p139)

In their review of the literature concerning studies which have attempted to ascertain the views of individuals with learning disabilities about changes in their lives (mainly the transition from more restrictive to less restrictive environments), Simons *et al.* (1991) similarly found that overall the studies reported that individuals wanted to leave the more restrictive settings and be resettled. The authors applaud the fact that there has been a significant increase between 1984 and 1989 of studies seeking users' views even though some of the studies have suffered from methodological difficulties. As they state:

> Perhaps the greatest significance of these developments is the acceptance, implicitly at least, that the views of people labelled as mentally handicapped (or at least those able to participate) constitute a valid perspective comparable with but distinctive from the perspectives of other actors involved: direct care staff, managers, relatives and even researchers. (p9)

Their review is also of interest for outlining the methods by which individual studies sought the views of clients, ranging from repertory grid procedures, through to interviewing by questionnaire, and the use of pictorial response formats, for example, faces showing a range of expressions denoting happiness or satisfaction (or otherwise) with aspects of one's life.

The aim, of course, of these techniques is to enable individuals with learning disabilities to express views even when they do not have the language skills to express their feelings.

Later we will discuss the use of similar procedures for clinical purposes but it is also worth referring here to the use of non-verbal techniques for assessment purposes. For many years researchers and practitioners have been attempting to develop self report measures in the field of learning disability as this form of assessment is common in other fields. Speake and Whelan (1977), for example, devised a choice box for educationally disadvantaged school leavers to use who were participating in work introduction courses.

As part of a job readiness battery, they were required to rate themselves on aspects related to work performance. The scale attempted to discover how the youngster saw himself as a worker and was entitled the Me at Work scale. It was in the form of questions and was answered by rating oneself on a seven point scale, only the two ends of which were labelled. The choice box was designed to take account of any problems there might be with reading or with verbal communication. The choice box consisted of seven lights, each with its own switch representing the seven positions on the scale. A separate reliability study on the scale used in conjunction with the choice box found the scale (apart from one item) to be reliable.

Other measures such as the Illustrated Vocational Inventory (Whelan and Reiter, 1980) and the Junior Interest Profile (Jeffree and Cheseldine, 1980) have also been developed in an attempt to overcome the difficulties clients have with reading and with verbal communication. Both of these measures enable pointing responses to be used in a forced choice format. In the interest section of the Illustrated Vocational Inventory, for example, the individual points to the job he is interested in from a pair of photographs depicting two different jobs. In all, 55 pairs of photographs are used, enabling a profile of interests across 11 job areas to be reported. In the Junior Interest Profile, the most desired leisure activity is pointed to on each page, from a set of four black and white drawings.

Thus, as may be seen, significant attention has been paid recently to giving a voice to individuals with all types of disability and to finding ways of seeking their views. The advocacy movement discussed later has also certainly put this notion firmly on the agenda. But if people are to increase their own personal effectiveness, what skills might be needed?

Many of the curriculum discussions over the past several years have tried to address this latter issue. One starting point which many researchers adopted was to look at studies of deinstitutionalisation. In these they examined which skills possessed by individuals seemed to lead to better adjustment to the community. Many interesting points emerged from such work.

Zisfein and Rosen (1984) for example, investigated the 'institutional personality', concluding that skills of an interpersonal nature were required by individuals in the community. In order to help prepare others for resettlement, they developed a personal adjustment training group counselling programme. The curriculum they developed was organised around five general goals:

1. The improvement in level of self regard, achievement of a realistic balance between aspirations and abilities, and the development of a heightened awareness of self as a social stimulus.
2. The reduction of acquiescent or submissive behaviour in response to coercive or exploitive attempts by others.
3. The reduction of patterns of helplessness, dependency and passivity and the learning of assertive responses.
4. The learning of self initiated problem solving behaviour.
5. The learning of appropriate heterosexual responses and the reduction of anxiety towards members of the opposite sex.' (p50)

These authors were amongst the earliest researchers to recognise the importance of interpersonal skills in the lives of people with learning disabilities and the need to develop problem solving skills if one is going to learn to cope. These are the skills, however, that often receive less attention in programmes of training. In the curriculum studies by Speake and Whelan (1985) it was found that individuals attending Adult Training Centres could acquire many self help skills provided they were taught with systematic teaching packages. However, there were steps even within these skills which caused difficulty. These were steps in the task analyses which required judgement or decision making. These more subtle skills are often at the core of interpersonal skills.

Unlike skills of a self help kind (dressing, bathing, washing etc.) or of a social academic nature (using a telephone, using a bus etc.), interpersonal skills do not lend themselves as readily to task analysis and to teaching by forward and backward training and systematic prompting. They are more difficult to teach and often require foresight and the ability to generalise across situations which we know can be more difficult for this client group.

In her review of the literature on follow up studies of adjustment to work, Speake (1978) found that work habits, skills and attitudes were important for successful adjustment to work as well as social skills, social competence and interpersonal skills. Factors related to the employer, and family and community support were also relevant.

Part of the challenge of community care and of helping individuals to take control over their lives is the need to help individuals to acquire such skills, to learn how to interact with others in mutually satisfying ways, to establish friendships, to communicate with others and to learn social skills. It is not enough to assume that placing individuals in a community provides access to that community. It may provide access to shops, to Post Offices and so on, but increasing personal effectiveness and taking control is also about gaining the skills necessary to settle into a community, to feel a part of it, to establish friendships.

In an interesting study conducted recently, Bees (1991) examined friendships in three groups of individuals: those living at home with families; those living in staffed houses in the community; and those from institutional settings. Five aspects of friendships were explored: size of friendship network, persistence over time, reciprocity, commitment and intimacy (Atkinson, 1987). Bees found a relationship between level of independent skill as measured by the Adaptive Behaviour Scale and size and quality of friendship networks, suggesting that skill development is an important focus.

Interestingly, for size of friendship network, community staffed homes did not produce better results than did institutional settings. Also, for all three groups, friendships with staff members played a large part in the network, but the quality of these relationships was lower in terms of the aspects of friendships referred to earlier than were friendships with other service users or with family members. In particular, elements of reciprocity were missing in the relationships with staff.

One of the conclusions reached by Bees from her research is the need to focus on training in social and interpersonal relationship skills and the role that staff have in this, both as 'trainers and facilitators'. Some of this is echoed by Raynes (1991), who also studied individuals living in residential facilities in the community. She found that, although houses were located close to amenities, the 'use of community amenities was uniformly low' and there was a 'degree of isolation which was striking in terms of the low level of contact with friends in the community'.

One of the other difficulties here is often that individuals living with the family have these family members as their main social contact. Adults with learning disability often socialise with parents long after most of us establish peer networks. Families also develop protective mechanisms and are reluctant to enable sons and daughters to participate in ordinary community activities, often preferring to help them to join special clubs and activity groups for individuals with learning disabilities.

Walsh, Coyle and Lynch (1988) in their 'Partners Project' attempted to widen the scope of activities of adults with learning disabilities by partnering individuals with young adults who could act as role models, and introduce new activities in a range of community based settings. The project achieved success whilst it was operational but subsequently there was no significant increase in any activity level compared to the situation prior to the project starting. They still spent a considerable amount of time at home watching TV, helping with household tasks or just sitting at home. However, the authors feel that the Project showed how important the need for companionship is in the lives of individuals with learning disability and that individuals with a learning disability value activities which are also valued by their peers.

So how can we create opportunities for individuals to be more effective? We need to reiterate the two main themes presented at the outset of this chapter, that of creating situations in which competencies can be improved and that of providing opportunities for individuals to have a say in their lives and to tell us how we can help them to improve the quality of their lives. Nothing has achieved this more dramatically than the self advocacy movement. This is an international movement in which people with disabilities have made their views known.

Flynn and Ward (1991) perceive the self advocacy movement as a large and transient network held together nationally and internationally by individuals and groups who are speaking to the non disabled world about their wishes and demands. The roots of the self advocacy movement can be traced through individual developments in Sweden, the USA, Canada, Australia and Britain and there are now well recognised themes and approaches in the messages that the movement is putting forward. It is possible to trace a path from the early and well meaning gentle encouragement of learning disabled individuals by others to the active involvement and empowerment of learning disabled people themselves. This path started with developments early in the 1960s, in the Swedish leisure clubs for people with learning disability in which a tradition began of the clubs being run by the individuals themselves. In Sweden, progress was then made to the provision of courses on decision making and committee organisation, to the point when in 1970 two conferences were held which signalled the beginnings of the self advocacy movement.

Although some people had been meeting with a self advocacy purpose in Omaha Nebraska since the 1950s, it was in the early '70s that North America accepted the baton of self advocacy with conferences in British Columbia and Oregon in 1974. This latter conference called itself People First and created a structure for all established groups to liaise with one another. By 1978, it had progressed to People First International. The significance of this was captured by Crawley (1982) in her review of the movement when she said: 'For the first time, opportunity has been generated for individuals to speak out and confer with peers in an environment of support'. Most recently there has been a conference in Manchester which launched a regional People First group and saw a huge promotional display of teeshirts, mugs, videos, books and pamphlets, all marketing the message that the advocacy movement is here to stay.

In Britain, Campaign for Mentally Handicapped People (CMH) took an initial lead with a number of participation events, the first culminating in the publication of *Our Life* (1972). Since this initial lead, a number of other participation events have taken place throughout the country. In the north west of England, participation events were initiated and funded by the North West Regional Training Team who encouraged a structure of residential workshops involving service users and service providers for the two to three day events. One such event took place in February 1991. It was attended by 23 people from South Manchester and resulted in the publication of a pamphlet entitled *Time for Talking* (1991).

In describing how the event evolved during the three days, the participants explained that by 'using pictures, symbols and drawings rather than words, we drew our feelings and wishes on to huge sheets of paper, talked them through and made plans'. What was also significant in this event was the learning experience it provided for professionals who are not used to expressing their own feelings in front of service users.

The service users who participated in this event, held at Brindle Lodge, discussed many aspects of their lives including their hopes and fears; where they live; where they work; what hurts and what helps; and what they wanted for the future. Often powerful pictures portrayed feelings that individuals were not able to express in words. What also emerged was that many of the participants were enabled to express themselves in ways in which they had never been able to do so before and many raw emotions were displayed. When the participants arrived at Brindle Lodge there were many fears being expressed, particularly 'I hope nobody laughs at me', 'Sometimes it's hard to understand everything' and 'People should listen'. These same individuals by the end of the event had been encouraged and enabled to make their views known by producing a charter stating what they wanted. The charter outlined the following areas:

- speak out and take control of our lives;
- home of my own;
- holidays;
- jobs and money;
- making friends.

What is also significant is that new groups emerged out of this experience (and others like it) and the participants themselves have gone on to presenting the results of the event to parents, managers, politicians, staff and professionals at conferences locally, receiving payment for their contribution. In the conclusion of their pamphlet (1991), the participants outlined what they had gained from having the opportunity to get together in such participation events. They stated that:

> Lots of us have stayed friends.
> We are getting listened to.
> The talk goes on and now we're putting words into ACTION.

As we have just highlighted, the advocacy movement has provided many individuals with some success in their lives, it has provided opportunities to be heard. However, many more people would benefit from this if recognition were given to the significant role that competency plays, as shown by the earlier quoted research. Many individuals who have so far taken advantage of the advocacy movement are those who have some skill in communicating with others and who have a degree of articulation.

In the earlier quoted Partners Project, Walsh *et al.* (1988) stated that 'It seems that various factors may discourage active participation in community life, such as: underestimation of an adult's level of competence; physical isolation; and a lack of opportunity to practise conversational skills'. The importance of communication skills cannot be underestimated, as we have seen from points made earlier in this book.

Participation requires that we develop programmes to enhance communication skills in other individuals who have not yet had such a voice or that we provide opportunities for others to speak on their behalf, for example through citizen advocacy. Crawley (1982) found that individuals participating in trainee committees needed to be taught the skills of working in a committee – how to set agendas, how to seek views, how to publicise decisions and so on. Crawley recommended programmes of training to enhance these skills and also suggested roles which staff members could play to facilitate the development of such skills.

Supported employment also has a role in creating opportunities for individuals to be more effective. Evans (1987), in reporting on the Waunfawr Venture as part of the ALL Wales Strategy, discussed the setting up of a project in which people with a learning disability could experience real work. Central to the project was the aim of integrating the workers into the local community and district by providing work opportunities in which individuals with learning disabilities could work alongside able-bodied locals on community projects. The goal was for individuals to succeed and thus failure experiences were minimised. Part of the eventual success of the project was deemed to be the interaction which was generated between the local community and the individuals with learning disabilities.

But effectiveness and control are not only about having a voice, participating in local communities and employment situations, but also about having feelings recognised and learning how to manage emotions. Increased attention is now being paid to the role of feelings in people's lives. Bailey *et al.* were stating in 1986 that 'The central challenge for the future is for us to gain a greater understanding of the feelings of people with mental handicaps'. Given the limited repertoire of verbal skills that many individuals with learning disabilities have, we often find that feelings are expressed through behaviours that staff members find hard to explain or that are labelled as 'challenging' or 'difficult' behaviours. Surely, many such behaviours must arise from the sheer frustration of not being able to express one's needs and feelings.

In their study identifying individuals whose behaviour challenges services, Speake *et al.* (1991) found that over 50 per cent of the individuals in the sample had no speech or could only use speech to meet their basic needs. For this sample of individuals there was also a correlation between high levels of dependency in functional abilities and a higher level of frequency of challenging behaviours.

Helping individuals to deal with the emotional side of their lives is a critical area in developing their personal effectiveness. Many individuals need help to deal with problems of concentration, restlessness, low attention span and other signs of high anxiety level. More recently, attention has been focused on the efficacy of using relaxation training in order to help individuals to overcome some of these difficulties. Lindsay and Baty (1986) for example, employed abbreviated progressive relaxation with four adults and used pulse rate and behavioural ratings to measure effectiveness. A consistent reduction was found over both measures for three out of the four subjects in the study.

In a later study, Lindsay and Kasprowicz (1987) showed a relaxation effect in ten subjects using a behavioural relaxation training procedure, a technique which 'concentrates on modelling both unrelaxed and relaxed behaviours in 10 areas of the body, and encouraging the individual to imitate the relaxed positions'. In carrying out the procedure the instructor gives manual guidance, uses prompts and provides feedback to the individual on his/her performance.

Another useful clinical tool is anger control therapy (Novaco, 1985), helping individuals to identify the triggers to their anger, recognising the bodily signs and symptoms of anger, learning techniques of relaxation and anxiety management and using self monitoring procedures to help individuals to cope with their feelings and to express them in more socially acceptable ways. Again, pictorial record forms depicting faces to chart moods and to record instances of anger can be very useful, providing individuals with the confirmation that their emotions are important, that they are not being ignored or having their feelings denied, and that they are engaged in intervention which will help them to deal better with their negative emotions.

Again, in dealing with problems of anxiety and lack of confidence, Lindsay and Kasprowicz (1987) used cognitive behaviour therapy as part of a larger research project with twenty adults with learning disabilities. They concluded in their article that the technique of challenging negative cognition was effective in helping individuals with problems in self confidence and low self esteem. They state that such problems interfere with the individual's ability to make really effective use of skills which have been learned and that new situations provoke anxiety because of the lack of self confidence.

Thus increasing effectiveness must be extended beyond helping people to acquire self-help skills to helping individuals to take control over their emotions, learn how better to express themselves and develop self confidence.

We stated at the outset that taking control was about skill development and about providing opportunities. We have tried to expand on these two topics in the last several pages. We would like to end this chapter by raising a few points which we feel are of concern to us as professionals working in the field of learning disability. We feel that there are some dilemmas that are thrown up by the issue of helping individuals to take more control over their lives and that these need to be acknowledged.

A very real issue is the one of protectionism versus risk taking. Walsh, Coyle and Lynch (1988) alluded to this in discussing their Partners Project. They found that some of the older parents expressed some concerns about participation, particularly their son/daughter using the bus and being out late at nights. In comparing the families, the authors concluded: 'By contrast, adults living at home whose families expressed any reluctance during the project took part in the least number of activities'. It is not easy for parents to take risks, especially when they have been the primary caregivers for a number of years, often with little support. Services, as well, often have to examine themselves and consider carefully the question of overprotection versus acceptable risk.

Many authorities are facing this vexed issued and are developing risk policies. One example is that of South Manchester. In drafting the policy on behalf of the authority, John and Eaton (1991) recognised that services also have difficulty in accepting risk and that what is needed is a framework to enable measured risk to be taken. They acknowledged that risk can never be completely eliminated in the human services but that from senior management downwards, policies and procedures can be outlined so that staff who work hands on can feel more comfortable, and carers can be assured that consideration has been given to all the variables involved in helping to achieve a level of independence in a responsible and justifiable way.

The risk policy outlines a procedure that ensures that staff consider each new risk situation and plan for it. Therefore, it provides largely unqualified staff with a structure and a safety net that has been agreed by the whole of the multidisciplinary team. Such policies are a very useful starting point in tackling this very real issue.

Another area of activity which can also throw up dilemmas is that of advocacy, a topic to which we are very committed and which we have discussed at some length already in this chapter. Space does not permit us to discuss the points at any length but practitioners in the field will recognise some of the following issues. Advocacy may be viewed by some as a new and trendy idea and therefore is in danger of being undertaken for the wrong reasons. As a 'politically correct' way of working, it can, ironically, create an unhealthy competition amongst some service providers, and may be used as a career springboard. The whole issue of advocacy may be cynically viewed by more traditional staff as another 'passing trend' rather than as a fundamental tenet of the way the services should be operating. The paradox sometimes occurs of self advocacy groups being staff led as opposed to staff supported, and sometimes, in the extreme, staff initiated without consultation with service users (you should have an advocacy group, therefore you will have an advocacy group!). Sometimes there is a misunderstanding of the fact that advocacy is a process, not necessarily an end in itself and that true self advocacy is a slow, awakening venture involving service users (often in joint collaboration with professionals) not a slick, speedy, or ready made package which offers cook-book solutions.

In a book whose theme is about taking control, we hope that this chapter has added to the enthusiasm about what is possible and reiterates that the time is now ripe for further development. We would like our own chapter to reflect on the effect that a small group of individuals have already had upon us and our professional practice. We are indebted to the South Manchester Brindle Lodge participation group and would like to end on something that they told us all:

> We want to be heard.
> We want to be listened to.
> We want to say what we think (with support).
> We want to Speak Out.

Chapter Ten

An Ordinary Life For Special People

Roy McConkey

> **Paradox** – statement apparently inconsistent or absurd yet really true; something conflicting with probability; apparent contradiction' (Penguin Dictionary).

People with disabilities can live ordinary lives. That's a paradox which few people in our society are prepared to believe, still less work to make happen. Pity and admiration are the most commonly expressed emotions about disability (Harris Poll, 1991). Pity . . . regret . . . grief for the life which has been spoilt; admiration . . . esteem . . . surprise at even their modest achievements. Little wonder then, people with disabilities feel patronised:

> The cripple is an object of Christian charity, a socio-medical problem, a stumbling nuisance and an embarrassment to the girls he falls in love with. He is pitied and ignored, helped and patronized, understood and stared at. But he is hardly ever taken seriously as a man. (Louis Batty, 1966).

The paradox is even more accentuated with mental handicap. For most people so labelled, their disabilities are not obvious – no wheelchairs, white sticks or hearing aids mark them out. Hence when they succeed in holding down a job or in passing their driving test, many claim that they were not really 'handicapped' in the first place! It is hard to live with a paradox.

Our services for adult persons with learning difficulties (mental handicap) have usually denied that any paradox exists. 'Special people require special services' has been their motto. Hence long-stay hospitals, social service hostels and adult training centres are still the dominant models of caring for people with moderate and severe handicaps. But latterly both statutory and voluntary services (Department of Health, 1991) are trying to embrace the ordinary life philosophy while continuing to meet their clients' special needs, by:

- using ordinary houses to accommodate small groups of men and women;
- availing of ordinary community services, such as GPs, dentists etc.;
- providing respite or foster care with ordinary families;
- enrolling clients to attend day and evening courses at Further Education Colleges or employment training schemes;
- encouraging their participation in ordinary leisure pursuits and making use of community recreational facilities;
- training and supporting clients to do ordinary jobs of work with local employers.

In terms of client satisfaction, these innovations are undoubtedly popular and they mark a major improvement on past models of caring. Towell (1988) described it as 'a shift away from segregated, ineffective and devaluing provision towards new services which provide opportunities and support for everyone to lead as normal a life as possible in the community'. But I am not sure that such innovatory services are any better at enabling people to have more control over their own lives; although they are a step in the right direction. Old service attitudes can be easily camouflaged in new jargon and surroundings.

In this chapter I shall examine some of the conditions needed for clients to become controllers, for staff to become servants and for managers to become redundant; at least as we know them! Such a revolution in services will not come quickly and it's arguable whether it can come at all. Living a paradox means keeping the tensions between ordinary and special in balance; conflicts of opinions in proportion; and disappointments about unfulfilled dreams in perspective.

Starting points

Ironically, the starting point is not with people who are labelled handicapped but rather it is with the beliefs and attitudes of the so called ablebodied. We are usually the power brokers; the decision takers and life makers of the people we care for, educate and train. Our beliefs about their disability, their potential to change and ultimately their worth to society will profoundly affect the style and content of our work.

Conceptions of disability

Defining 'mental handicap' is fraught with difficulties. As I have argued elsewhere (McConkey, 1992), the label is best conceived as a social categorisation that conveys an entitlement to services rather than one which describes personal characteristics. Hence Marc Gold's parody of definitions using hypothetical constructs of intelligence and social adaptation remains for me the best summary of what it means to have a mental handicap, namely they are people who are fully human but '...whose level of functioning requires from society significantly above average training procedures and superior assets in adaptive behaviour manifested throughout life' (Gold, 1976). Until such times – if ever – as geneticists can transplant chromosomes, surgeons can correct deficits in brain functioning and biochemists can regulate the performance of the central nervous system, there is little to be gained by speculating on biological explanations for this disability or searching for miracle cures. Rather the emphasis has to be on producing training programmes and social adaptations in the belief that these will ultimately minimise the handicaps and enable these people to function age-appropriately in our society.

However I doubt if this belief is shared across professionals, service administrators and families although, significantly, most self-advocates express their disability in terms of the help they need – 'I feel I'm not as bright as other people might be. But at the same time, I think we should be allowed to have the chances others have in their lives' (Lundstrom-Roche, 1981).

Potential for change

Linked with conceptions of disability are beliefs about people's potential to change and the conditions which best stimulate it. Ideally, objective data about people's progress would replace speculation and reduce disputes, but so little research has been undertaken that this Utopia is unlikely to arise in our lifetime. Indeed we have hardly begun to identify the influences which mould staff's beliefs, such as their past experiences with the client and with similar clients; opinions expressed by their manager and other staff; their training and previous work situations; their own upbringing and values, and so on.

The belief that people can change is fundamental to the success of every intervention we make, be it toilet-training, reducing challenging behaviours or resettling people from institutional to community living. But it is harder for many people to accept that progress may only start if they change the way in which they interact with the person, or make changes to the person's environment – 'It is the client who should change, not me'. Hardest of all is to continue believing that change is still possible when so little progress is evident after all the efforts which have been made.

Worth to society

How are the millions of pounds spent each year on services for people with severe learning difficulties to be justified? In an increasingly competitive 'social care' market, our arguments will need to be well marshalled. Statements of rights, enshrined in law, are an important safeguard.

> Disabled people, whatever the origin, nature and seriousness of their handicaps and disabilities, have the same fundamental rights as their fellow citizens of the same age, which implies first and foremost the right to enjoy a decent life, as normal and as full as possible. (United Nations Declaration on The Rights of Disabled Persons, 1975).

But such statements will not satisfy the sceptics who say Why bother? Possible responses include

– how would you feel if it was you or a family member who was disabled;
– what kind of society would result from ignoring or exterminating the disabled;
– people with disabilities are a positive force for good in our society in that they help communities retain important values such as compassion, gentleness and patience; and
– what right have you to say that your life is any more worthwhile to society than that of another person?

The three issues identified above – conceptions of disability, potential for change and worth to society – merit much more contemplation and discussion than they have received to date in our residential and day services for adult persons. Mission statements are incomplete if they do not spell out the beliefs which underpin them.

This debate must also embrace parents and family carers as well as including the wider community, especially local and national politicians who ultimately determine policies and funding.

Needless to say, self-advocates must be to the fore in these discussions; they have to claim control over their lives and convince the sceptics that they can cope. A useful starting point is for professionals and parents to listen to the aspirations of older teenagers and young adults as they prepare to leave school or college – to have a job of work, a home of their own and the company of friends (Lunstrom-Roche, 1981):

> 'I'd like to work in a hotel, in catering or a hall porter something in that line.'
> 'I'd like to try having my own house. I could always come home at weekends.'
> 'I'd like to get married – I have a girlfriend already.'

Do we believe that special people can live ordinary lives?

Serving individuals

'People think that we're all the same, but we're not all the same.' The astute comment of a Dublin lady working in sheltered employment is so true yet there is no surer way of robbing people of their individuality than by treating them as one of a group – the 'mentally handicapped'.

Institutional life in mental handicap hospitals provided the most extreme examples. Wards of 'patients' shared a common wardrobe of clothes, they queued to be toileted and bathed as the staff commanded; they were given no choice of food or mealtimes and they could be moved around the hospital as beds were needed (Ryan, 1980). Under-staffed and ill-equipped establishments end up herding rather than caring for people. Sad to say this legacy lingers on for nearly 30,000 British citizens who are still resident in mental handicap hospitals, albeit with the worst excesses trimmed off.

Tailoring services to individuals rather than expecting them to fit into whatever service is available is such a radical shift in policy that the ramifications, still less the repercussions, have yet to be worked through. What, then, are the indicators of an individual-led service, be it residential or day service, respite care or educational provision? Among the characteristics I would list are the following.

Terminology

What names are used to describe the people being served and the people employed to serve them? A national survey of day centres in Ireland found that 'trainees and instructors' were the most popular terms but others included 'residents and supervisors', 'students and educators'; and 'clients and attendants' (McConkey and Murphy, 1989).

The names we choose both signal and determine the relationships between the servers and the served, hence they need to be selected carefully and regularly reviewed. No one term will suffice for all staff or all service-users. Job titles should reflect the primary function which staff are expected to fulfil, for instance 'houseparent' or 'home help' imply quite different roles. Likewise, service-users could variously be described as 'students', 'trainees' and 'tenants' as the service context changes from college, to work placements, to home. Be warned though; changing names but not service practices is a deception widely practised of late! 'By their fruits shall ye know them!'

For a truly individual-led service the solution is obvious: simply call people by their names and not by their labels! But is the service sufficiently small so that all staff – from the top-managers down – know every service-user by name and vice versa? And what forms of address are used within the service – is it first names or formal titles, do they vary for staff and service-users? The nature of our relationships is expressed in these small, yet so important ways.

Possessions

Personal possessions help to define our individuality. Are people with learning difficulties encouraged to choose their own clothes? Have they a room of their own which they can decorate and arrange to their taste? And how much freedom have they to spend their money on what they want? Pertinent questions for families as well as care staff to ponder on.

In residential settings, what furniture and fittings, if any, belong to the occupants? If they were to move to their own accommodation what could they take with them? Do they have any tenancy rights to their present accommodation or could they be dispossessed of it if management so decides? Likewise in day centres, what actually belongs to the attenders? Are they allocated sole use of certain facilities as per 'staff rooms'? In sum, what can people with learning difficulties call their own? Because from ownership comes control.

Individual plans

The value of individual written plans is now well-attested in education and in social services generally and in some countries, such as the United States, they have become mandatory. These plans help to ensure that an individual's specific needs have been identified and that proposals are made to meet those needs. Regular reviews of the plans (at least annually) should promote service accountability (Humphries *et al.* 1985).

In my experience, the impact of individual planning is enhanced if:

(1) The service-user is actively engaged in the process; in preparatory meetings and when the final plan is being drawn up. Although this is not easy with a minority of people who have marked difficulties in communication, this should not preclude others from contributing.

(2) The people who have most contact with the individual are directly involved in drawing up the plan. Visiting professionals may facilitate the process and give advice but the front-line service workers and their users have to own the plans.

(3) The review meeting brings together all the people involved with the individual – family or residential staff; education or day service staff; volunteer helpers etc. At the very least this ensures an exchange of information; at best it leads to coordinated planning across service settings.

(4) Named people are made responsible for implementing the plans. In residential or day services, each member of staff can act as a 'key-worker' for a small number of clients; taking a particular interest in them as people and making it easier for family or community contacts to link with the service.

(5) Service managers are party to the decisions so that the necessary resources are provided more quickly. Arguably one of the prime responsibilities of any service manager is to ensure that the users' needs are met; hence managers are in an ideal position to convene review meetings.

Operating such review systems for large numbers of service users can be very demanding on already over-stretched staff. Computer technology can assist in notifying people of meetings and in recording and analysing needs across clients within the services.

Consultations

What mechanisms exist within the service for users to be consulted before decisions are made? For example:

- Are there regular house meetings for the residents, a committee of attenders at the Social Education Centre or a student council for senior pupils in secondary schools or in FE Colleges?
- What opportunities are provided for service-users to became more adept at the skills needed for this sort of Committee work?
- Is there a specified procedure by which users can register any complaints or grievances? Are they given opportunities to appraise the performance of staff who work with them?
- What topics are users consulted about? Judicious selection can render impotent even the best of systems. Among the most contentious issues, I suspect, are involving users in selecting new staff and giving them a say when making decisions about spending cuts.

Similar questions about consultation can rightly be asked of how management deal with front-line staff because their example often dictates how staff consult with service users, if at all.

Preferences and choices

For people with learning difficulties many of our services were designed on a 'take-it-or-leave-it' basis, reflecting the charitable ethos from which they sprung. Moreover, any choice of service was frequently dictated by the person's perceived abilities rather than his or her preferences. Hence more able people were moved out of hospitals into community settings if they were judged capable of being able to cope; whereas others were left behind even though they preferred to move.

But many adults with learning difficulties are still denied a choice in even the small decisions of home life. Do they choose the food they eat, the programmes they watch on television, the time they go to bed or when they take a bath? Some parents and professionals impose their routines on everyone in the house.

In schools or day centres, what choices can students and attenders make about the activities in which they participate and the people with whom they do them? Some days, can they choose to do nothing? And if it is said that they are not capable of deciding for themselves, what are we doing to help them to learn?

Negotiating a compromise between people's preferences and actual possibilities is an art which many service personnel and users still have to master. Mistakes invariably occur – the man with Down's Syndrome who overestimated his competence to hold down a job in the café, or the lady whose parents were convinced she could not cope with using public transport but she proved them wrong. But in both cases, the man and the woman had the opportunity to try.

The real difficulty comes with family or service systems which are so rigid that people are denied the chance of a trial so that their preferences and the possibilities for change are never tested.

Range of service options

People labelled as having learning difficulties have many diverse needs which change over time so that no one service can ever meet everyone's needs for all time – hence the failure of institutional care. Instead a range of service options is needed. Residential provision must span 24 hour nursing care for the most dependent, supported accommodation with sleep-in staffing for those who could not cope alone and staff support available during waking hours or on a visiting basis. Various forms of independent living arrangements – from shared tenancies to owner occupancy – complete the range (Brown, 1988).

Post-school day-time provision must be equally diverse, embracing special developmental units for the most severely impaired, further education courses, employment training, paid work and opportunities for community participation in leisure pursuits (Seed, 1988).

As yet very few districts in the United Kingdom offer the necessary range of residential, respite care and day service provision. Moreover the demand for places in residential and day services usually exceeds the number available. The consequence is that people often are misplaced into whatever service is available rather than receiving the one they most need. Resources rarely match the rhetoric of policy statements about choice and matching services to needs.

Encouraging initiatives

Finally, does the family or the service encourage individual initiatives? Are people given the chance to solve their own problems if difficulties arise and are they encouraged to experiment, to try other ways? Often parents and staff take over the 'task' when they perceive the person to be failing and they are happier to stick with familiar routines.

Likewise are people with learning difficulties given responsibility for chores around the home, school or centre and do we expect the same level of performance from them as we would from the able-bodied worker?

In teaching people to do 'jobs', do we aim to develop their autonomy by encouraging them to check their work and to monitor their speed and accuracy. Admittedly we have much to learn about how best to do this but unless we do, people will remain dependent on their instructors.

Service tensions

The ultimate goal of services based on ordinary life principles is for the clients to outgrow their need for help, to become ordinary members of society. This has become a reality in recent years for a growing number of men and women with learning difficulties as they take over the tenancies of their own homes, obtain paid employment, enjoy an active social life in their community and fall in love and marry.

At the other extreme are a small minority of people whose disabilities are so severe that they are totally dependent on other people to care for all their personal needs and for getting around; they may show little reaction to a change in surroundings and they appear unable to communicate with other people. For them, special help will always be required albeit in as normal a setting as possible.

By far the largest group, though, are those who fall between these extremes, unable to cope without help and yet aspiring to lead ordinary lives. The tensions between self-control and service-control are likely to be most pronounced here. As I have noted above, services which are geared to meeting the needs of individuals are better able to cope with these tensions as they share decision-making with their users and encourage them to take greater control over the own lives. However, even they are not immune from the tensions which arise from the paradox of special people living ordinary lives.

In this section I want to explore some specific tensions which frequently arise in residential and day services for adult persons and, where possible, give some pointers as to how best professional service personnel might cope. There are however no guaranteed solutions and I doubt if there ever will be.

Conflicts between parents' wishes and those of their sons and daughters

People with learning difficulties living in the family home often experience the same tensions as do adolescents, albeit at a later age and with less aptitude for persuading reluctant parents. Staff often label parents as 'overprotective', especially of their daughters (Walsh, 1988).

The tension is greatest when it comes to decisions about the person leaving the family home. Suggestions made by Richardson and Ritchie (1986) for helping parents at this time can be applied to other transitions from childhood to adulthood.

> There would be enormous benefit in involving parents (as well as handicapped people themselves) in the planning of residential care . . . Our research leads us to argue for a wide range of provision . . . in order to accommodate the individual needs of people with mental handicaps and to provide some choice for parents . . . most parents' knowledge of existing provision is sketchy and as often as not based on uncertain rumour. Few know what their local authority's policies are . . . Parents could be given valuable support through involvement with a parents' support group.

The key words are involvement, choice, information and support. Family contact must be maintained throughout the school years and beyond, a feature that is notably lacking in much of our existing provision.

Responsibility and risk taking

The legal status of people with learning difficulties is very unclear, especially as to whether or not they can be held responsible for their own actions (Bayliss, 1987). For example, would staff be considered negligent if a resident of a group home was knocked down the first time she went unaccompanied to the shops; who pays for the repairs to a neighbour's car damaged in a fit of temper by an attender at a day centre?

Ensuring that the service has adequate insurance cover does not remove the tensions involved for staff in risk-taking. Managerial support is essential, as are explicit policy guidelines along with the involvement and support of families if appropriate. But to eliminate risk is to prevent people from living and learning.

138

Self-advocacy

People with physical and sensorial disabilities have rightly promoted self-advocacy within services. For men and women with learning difficulties this is particularly challenging as many have problems in communicating and in understanding. If people are reliant on staff support in advocacy, can we be sure that it is their wishes and not those of the staff which are being expressed? Is there a danger that the most vocal service-users are foisting their opinions on their peers? What sanctions can self-advocates invoke if their views are ignored?

When services encourage greater self-advocacy they are likely to increase rather than to lessen tensions, but is there a choice if service-users are to gain greater control over their lives? Experiences over the past decade have identified ways of nurturing self-advocacy from school-days onwards (Sutcliffe, 1990).

Staff turnover

The quality of any social service is determined largely by the people working in it. Their qualifications, experience and personality all contribute to producing a 'good' staff team – an elusive mixture that cannot be created to order. Our new style of services places even greater demands on staff talents as they strive to cope with clients' physical, social and emotional needs.

An ever-present tension within services is that arising from staff changes. A recent study of small community residences in the United States reported turnovers in excess of 50 per cent within one year (Larson and Lakin, 1992). Among the reasons often given are low wages, poor job satisfaction among staff and little prospect of career advancement.

I suspect that for the foreseeable future, services will have to live with this phenomenon and hence will need to evolve strategies which minimise the disruption caused to service-users by staff changes through detailed induction procedures; clear policy guidelines; regular supervision and guidance; and ongoing training and development. Unfortunately our health and social services have a very poor record on supporting staff in these ways and old attitudes are hard to change even when money is made available for doing this.

Sexuality

Issues about sexuality invariably create tensions as people take more control over their own lives. Can the young man living in staffed accommodation invite his girlfriend to spend the night in his room? Is a homosexual relationship between two apparently consenting young adults permissible within a group home? Should married couples be discouraged from having children?

Education and counselling must be available to both staff and service-users to counter ignorance and to aid informed decision-making while preserving privacy and confidentiality. There are no simple, ready-made solutions and services often have to evolve fresh responses to the particular circumstances that arise with individuals. As yet, few professionals feel equipped to tackle these issues so they are too frequently 'brushed under the carpet'. Hopefully the growing literature on this topic will foster a more explicit service response (Craft, 1991).

Balancing needs equably

Funding for services will never be sufficient to meet all the needs of people with learning difficulties. How then are service providers to balance different people's needs in a way which is equitable and yet enables their users to have control? This circle does not square.

For example, four people have happily shared a group home; one person dies suddenly and the service wants to offers the vacant place to a man living in the family home who needs looking after as his elderly mother is seriously ill. The existing residents are reluctant to have a 'stranger' come to their home and say so forcefully. What is to happen? Negotiations might continue; alternatives might be sought and compromises might be found. Invariably the process will be fraught with tensions and in many instances the weaker party – the users – will become the losers.

Leadership styles

Which brings me neatly to the crucial role of leadership style within services. Given the characteristic of the new style of services I have described, it is obvious that we need leaders who know their service-users personally and are familiar with their needs; who are willing to consult and listen to the views of front-line staff and users; who are prepared to try new ways and take risks; who are ready to negotiate and seek compromises and, of course, do all this within cash-limited budgets.

Few managers could ever live up to such high ideals but what is most worrying is that our present management systems in health and social services are so hierarchical and directive that they can never nurture this new style of leadership until they alter radically their long established style of operating. Unless they do, staff and users will endure considerable tensions as they try to grapple with a system that at best only pays lip-service to their aspirations.

One solution is to move away from large bureaucratic service structures towards smaller, more autonomous agencies, with discrete functions and their own budgets (Towell, 1988). Hence I welcome the growth of voluntary agencies as service providers, a model which has served most countries well in developing local services.

Talk of revolutions

Enabling people with learning difficulties to lead ordinary lives and encouraging them to take more control of their lives is a revolution which has only just begun. It is too early to assess its chance of success and still less to predict all its outworkings if it were to became a reality. The goal, though, could not be simpler – to give every person the opportunity for a decent life, as normal and as full as possible.

Equally clear is the mechanism by which this will, or will not, happen, namely the attitudes, talents and styles of the staff in services or the family members who look after their relative. Existing training procedures, job descriptions and support mechanisms will need to be radically changed during the revolution.

Finally, the powerhouse for the revolution must came from the people who stand most to benefit – the persons with learning difficulties. Are they up to the task? Are we preparing them for the task?

Mahatma Gandhi (1948) wrote, 'a non-violent revolution is not a program of seizure of power. It is a program of transformation of relationships, ending in a peaceful transfer of power'. Transforming the relationships between the helper and the helped, the teacher and the taught, is the solution to the paradox of enabling special people to lead ordinary lives.

Chapter Eleven

In the Family

(a) Promoting Choice and Self Regulation for People with Learning Difficulties

Mary and Christopher Lodge

From the very earliest days of Christopher's life we (his immediate family) were aware of the formative nature of personal choice; although at the time this amounted to giving him the same sort of upbringing as that of his elder brother and sister. They were four years old and six years old when he was born in 1966.

When Christopher was three days old, we were given a pessimistic prognosis of the likely achievements of a person with Down's Syndrome by the family doctor, who was clearly upset. We were given contradictory advice and opinions by the health visitor and others who turned up at the house in the following days. These ranged from 'In a more ordinary family he wouldn't be noticed' to 'He will become the centre of interest in the family'. We filtered out the less useful advice, but took note of some pointers, which were often at the back of our minds as Christopher and his brother and sister developed.

One of the important pointers was the implication, for the family unit, of a member who might become the centre of interest. This would clearly be unfair, and a cause of jealousy, so we were on our guard against the possibility. A second pointer was provided by Rex Brinkworth (who had just started his research into the education of children with Down's Syndrome). He stressed the importance of exposing the child to as much sensory stimulation as possible, even to the extent of waking him up and making him play with us – quite against the usual family procedure of 'let sleeping babies lie'! He also advised us to give Christopher opportunities to make personal choices as soon as he could indicate a wish in any way. An example of this early educative procedure is that from a very early age, when I put Christopher to bed, I would tuck in the bedclothes, ask 'Shall I turn the light off?' and wait for some kind of response. When he was very young he used to nod from a supine position. As he developed a certain amount of fear of the dark, he changed his response to 'No!' I would then leave it on, and turn it out when he was asleep. He must have woken in the night at some time and realised that he had not quite got his message across to me. From then on he negotiated for some form of night light to remain on all night. He has always required this form of security, and in any new or temporary sleeping accommodation will carefully suss out the possibilities and explain to the other persons involved what light he hopes they will agree to keep on. If this is not possible, he has been able to accept a torch instead, for instance on school camping trips. By studying Christopher in the family setting we gradually set up a system of planned learning through self-advocacy, which meant that Christopher could be assisted to reach his full potential, while the rest of the family could also reach theirs. We were determined that no member of the family should be impeded by their blood relationship to a person with learning difficulty. On the other hand, we expected them to take every opportunity to help and encourage him.

On the basis of this philosophy, we all treated Christopher as a member of a normal five-person family. He was given an equal chance with his brother and sister to have his needs considered, but it was made clear that they might not always be met exactly as he wished. At first this was only understood by the other four family members, but as he grew up he began to understand the situation, by means of example and careful explanation. Based on the premise of fairness, decisions about family activities considered everyone's welfare; the family debated what activities could be done together, what required separate groupings and whose turn it was to choose (a vital concept in our family). An example of how this worked in practice was in the domestic area. Our daughter had a very keen eye for demarcation issues and sexual discrimination, well before it was enshrined in the statute book. She made sure that the male members of the household took equal turns in all the communal chores required for the efficient running of a busy household. Christopher's ability was ascertained and he was given his responsibilities; his first job was laying the table for the evening meal. He could not count reliably at this early stage, but I used my knowledge of task analysis to assist him to pull his weight. My method was to place one chair and placemat at the table and ask him to get a knife,fork and spoon for himself and put them on the table. I then placed another chair and placemat, asked him to put out the cutlery for me, and so on, until each person present was catered for. This of course took time and patience, but it was worthwhile when he was able to say 'I did that!' with a blissful appearance of righteousness, and receive formal recognition of his efforts from the rest of the family. In this way he gradually learned to do various tasks in the home, including making his own bed. To a friend who said she always made her sons' beds because they did not do it well enough, I commented 'Well they have to lie on the beds, so it's up to them to get it right!' As a result of his willingness, as opposed to his actual skill, Christopher was seen to be pulling his weight by his siblings, and gained status and rights within the family which he himself could understand.

Christopher was therefore gradually empowered to make his needs known and to have them considered on their merits, because he had something to offer in the way of bargaining counters, that is, performance of his duties within the home to the best of his ability. The first use he made of his ability to bargain effectively was seen when he wanted to watch television, which, as it was not in the living room, required leaving the vicinity of jobs to be done. He would state that he was going to watch the children's programmes (from about 4.30–6.00). We, on the other hand, would say 'Have you laid the table for supper yet?' as we knew he would not be willing to leave the last ten minutes of the programme to get the job done by 6.00p.m. He would mutter under his breath about this, until he understood that it was a question of timing, not an easy concept for a person with learning difficulty. He also understood that when he had done it he could relax without fear of interruption of his enjoyment.

This type of give and take situation is a normal part of family life but, in the case of a child with learning difficulty, becomes more obviously a teaching and learning opportunity. The main problem for a person of limited intelligence is generalisation of learning, so a very firmly established routine is an aid to orderly thinking.

The other normal part of family life, communicating (involving both listening and speaking), was also an essential part of this training. Christopher soon understood the importance of verbalising what he had done in the way of domestic duties and going on to verbalise his expectation of his right to watch the children's programmes. The effect of these routines of action and verbalisation was to facilitate his awareness of himself and others. Many years later we became familiar with the movement for self-advocacy, and realised that Christopher had most of the necessary skills already. In his case, self-advocacy was facilitated by his gift for communicating. He had learned to use his knowledge of his family's preferences in order to negotiate times and places for his own interests. He would get out the Radio Times after the evening meal and point out a gardening programme, which he would be at pains to explain that I could watch early in the evening, and that he would be watching Dallas after that. Again, this ability to persuade through an understanding of other people's needs, as well as his own, was won through listening to the same sort of negotiations going on amongst the rest of the family. Christopher has gone on from this level of self-advocacy to being a representative of others with less ability than himself. His former experience in the family is of use when he represents his friends in the CARE organisation where he now lives. When I asked him if he could write something about self-advocacy, I was in the middle of an explanatory sentence when he said: 'I know! I know, all about that!' He then sat down and wrote the enclosed account of his day at the CARE conference in 1991. It is re-typed literally from his draft, with only small grammatical corrections such as 'having a girl friend' for 'have a girl friend', and of spelling 'reversals' such as 'problems' for 'probelms'.

Christopher's account of advocacy at CARE

I packed my night bag to go to Leicester for the CARE Conference. It was a long way from Ironbridge.

What we did at the Conference

On Wednesday afternoon everyone had tea and coffee and a biscuit and then it was time to sit down and listen to other CARE communities what they say at the conference, like workshops, social activities and satellite homes and what is changed in the CARE community.

We have four residents at the conference and we speak in order. First one was Penny: she talked about the history of Ironbridge and what it was like to live there and how do you like the CARE community when you moved there. The next was Richard and he talked about social activities. We go out swimming and we go to club and we go shopping at Telford and we go to college in the morning or the evening and the afternoon. We do what we like at the weekends, like we go to the pub for a drink or go to church and we have a big cinema at Telford with ten films to see. The next was Peter and he talked about workshops we have in the CARE community and how we like to work there with him. I was talking about satellite homes.

Then we had a break to talk, and a drink and then we went back in the living room to talk about health and safety, what you do in your cottage. We have health and safety at your workshop,like woodwork and laundry, kitchen and we have a garden and don't forget the maintenance.

When we talked about this conference in our community hall at Ironbridge, everyone listened to what we say about it. Someone organised this meeting, it was Kerry, one of our staff and she was chosen to look after us, what we did with our speeches; she helped us to write it down. And then we read them to tell the others, and they ask questions if they want to. I had a piece of paper to write down the residents' votes for satellite homes:

18 said 'Yes'

7 said 'No'

2 said 'I don't know'

Then we talk about relationships and then talk about care for other people and why they call us mentally handicapped people because not everyone likes it so try and stop it as soon as they can.

At our cottage we talk about having a girlfriend and a boyfriend and I think it is very good by love. So you can solve your problems out and do what you like. When someone sits alone you can have a talk or kiss, but one thing you can't do in the cottage is hug or kiss in the lounge. If you do you will get jealousy with other residents. The place to use is the quiet room.

(b) His Right to Choose

Angela Jones, Mother of Gavin

I wonder if you would be prepared to give a demonstration of breast-feeding to the next wave of mothers-to-be? Gavin certainly is a bonny baby and his feeding and weight gain are excellent. I'm sure they would all benefit from watching you both! You can imagine how pleased I felt to be told this – a new mum down at the baby clinic every Thursday afternoon.

However, during the next few months, Gavin didn't quite reach the expected milestones at the same rate as the others. It took five months for us to query the 'normality' of our child and another five months for the health authority to agree that there was a problem.

During a time of anxiety, delay can be a crippling frustration you can well do without. To try and overcome this, my husband John and I busied ourselves by absorbing information in an area neither of us knew anything about. There followed a period of several months during which time we read leaflets, articles, authoritative books, consulted dictionaries and questioned experts; experts in this case being those who had experienced a similar situation and had survived, namely, other parents.

Our searching led us to a remarkable guide who, through the next few years' was to lead us through the minefield. She was a physiotherapist who had developed an astute perception of her craft. She had spent a lifetime working with children with severe difficulties, but had retained a sufficiently open mind to enable her to try new solutions to recurring problems. Under her direction, we began to look again at this small child who was apparently able to do so little. She taught us how to view him from a new perspective, a positive one. We stopped listing those things which he couldn't do, the approach taken by the health service at that time, and instead devised a list of everything he could do. This gave us a completely new set of criteria upon which to base goals to work towards. The impact which this had on the family was wonderful. No longer passive bystanders, hampered by frustration and lack of information, we were now able to do something practical and 'hands-on'. In our situation, as it was then, this can be very therapeutic. Slowly, we began to feel back in control and, perhaps more importantly, we did not have to endure the prolonged delays offered by the medical professionals, on whose every word we had come to rely.

The overall goal, set at the beginning, was to help Gavin to be in control of as much of his world as possible. If this meant no more than learning to sit upright, then so be it. But one thing was certain, Gavin was going to be helped to develop those skills which he lacked, to enable him to exert some degree of control in his life. Having embarked upon a programme designed specifically for him, we found that the more he achieved, the more control we wanted to help him to achieve. As we progressed, we learned to keep the goals general rather than specific, so that we wouldn't fall into the trap of over-estimating objectives and falling short. Disappointment was something that neither we nor those who helped us needed at that time. Instead we took the view that every success was an unexpected bonus and the difference this made to our morale was amazing.

Once we recognised the need for a new approach, we began to think differently about Gavin. As we worked with him, we very quickly came to realise that the fact he was progressing, however slowly, meant that he really was capable of learning, which was something we had initially questioned.

Before he was five, John and I had realised that at some point in the future, possibly in his middle teens, Gavin would probably leave the family and live in residential accommodation. To this end, we set about gradually preparing the family for such a departure. So, the goal became clearer. We had to help Gavin to become as independent as possible so that, in the future, he could live with as much dignity as possible. Somehow, we had to ensure that he would be able to exercise his right to choose, to make decisions as far as he was able. Regardless of the type of community in which he would eventually live, Gavin would take his place in the world, we were sure of that.

As a young child, Gavin often appeared to be uncomfortable in his environment. With hindsight, we believe that this was the result of distorted sensory input, visual, auditory and touch (we were unable to determine the effect of taste and smell). As we had been taught how to 'look' and make observations, our conclusions, gathered over a period of time, were put together to produce a remediation package.

The first result, and one of the swiftest we had, was a change in the way Gavin used his hands. At the age of twenty-two months, both were covered with bright red lines and were closing up with lack of use. To open them, we drew them, palms open, on a vinyl surface for a few minutes each day. At the end of three weeks, they began to open, soon were flexing and before long, Gavin learned how to pick up and later to hold objects. This ability to hold an object meant that many years later Gavin would hold his own fork and control his own feeding, a giant step, if not for mankind, then at least for Gavin!

Another equally important step forward came later and took much longer. Having decided that Gavin had a hearing problem but definitely was not deaf, we set about trying to identify the problem. After much investigation, several experiments, much laughter from us and many tears from Gavin, we concluded that his hearing problem was a hypersensitivity to high frequency noise. In order to raise his tolerance of the offending sound, it was necessary to 'bombard' him with as much of it as we could conjure up. This whole process took eighteen months, but at the end of that time Gavin was able to sit close to someone who was tearing paper, or even hear chips frying, without bursting into tears. He was now ready to participate comfortably in family activities. Many years further on, he enjoys sounds, particularly music and he is able to ask to have the television put on, whereas once it distressed him. Of course, now, having developed quite a sense of humour, Gavin is often seen giggling himself silly at any unusual, particularly 'rude' sounds (little did we think all those years ago)!

During the time that Gavin was developing tolerance of sound, he was also being introduced to other types of sensory input to try to combat difficulties which gradually became evident. For example, because the muscles in his top lip did not seem to function, drinking was difficult, so we started work on that. Then there was a problem with his handling of various textures, so we had a look at that. But most important of all was his vision. He could see, we were sure of that, but he couldn't move his eyes without turning his head. Seeing this as restrictive, we started working with basic tracking exercises. If we needed any proof that what we were doing was right, it came unexpectedly twelve months later. Gavin, at that time, was seen by an ophthalmologist who, after examining him, declared that if we had not done our remediation when we had, Gavin would shortly have been partially-sighted. Apparently he does not have binocular vision and, with lack of use, his brain would just have shut down the unused eye. Hearing this, we and our team set about his continuing programme with renewed enthusiasm and determination.

Perhaps the most outstanding result of all this input was an incident which occurred when Gavin was three and a half years old. It also served as probably the most important lesson that I learned during this entire time. Gavin's younger sister Anna had been born eighteen months before, able to absorb and feed back information in a manner which, it seemed to us at the time, was absolutely unique and totally amazing! Her speed of learning was a constant source of wonder to us and the fact that she could take in, retain and give back data, thrilled us. It has to be said at this point that, after three years of trying, without success, to get Gavin to identify objects, I had stopped, believing that perhaps he was just unable to make the connections.

So, with the children aged three and a half and one and a half, we were visiting friends one afternoon when I, in the role of besotted mother wanting to show off my super-duper whizz-kid daughter, asked Anna to show our friends where the light was. She immediately looked towards the ceiling, but before she could indicate, Gavin raised his arm and pointed to the light from his seat on the floor. I was stunned. He had never done anything like it before and I had no idea he even knew what a light was. He was to prove me wrong many times in the years that followed, but the lesson learned on that day has never been forgotten.

Looking back, I realise that it was a long time before Gavin took control over any part of his universe. For the first five years of his life we had only occasional glimpses of him exerting control, but as he became older, developed skills and found applications for them, life began to change for him.

We thought we were prepared for Gavin's move away from the family, but it came about six years prematurely and, at first, we neither recognised the need nor were ready for it. He was eleven and a half years old and our calculations were badly out. We thought it would happen mid-teens, because of his size and our inability to handle his weight. This was not the case. Developmentally, he had grown beyond our skills and we had not seen it. So, in order to find an alternative environment for him, we looked at what was available. Finally, we found a superb establishment, only twelve miles away from home, which was near enough for us to feel that we could retain an element of involvement in his management. It also meant that he would continue to attend the same school, a factor at the top of the agenda when making our decision. At the beginning, there was no guarantee that it would work out. Fortunately, both school and those around us were very supportive during this period, which helped enormously. But it was not long before we realised that it wasn't Gavin who was having a problem accepting the new regime, it was his parents!

Previously I had said that Gavin would probably never move himself in his wheelchair; he certainly had never shown any inclination to do so with us. But, in his new home, it took just three weeks for him to propel himself forwards. Granted, it took another eighteen months to perfect angles, obstacles and corners, but in the meantime he had gained a freedom and independence he had never known before. Of course, when your friends, plus a cup of tea, are on the other side of the room, then motivation increases and there is suddenly an urgency in the need to move from A to B.

Four years ago, Gavin's school, in conjunction with ourselves, set a long term goal for him, namely, 'to assist Gavin to control his environment'. At the time it sounded to me like a textbook ambition. But in the last two years, we have seen him do just that and it is an experience which is difficult to describe in words. This young man, who, as a small child needed so much stimulation at all levels, is now indicating his wants and needs, enjoying shared periods of concentration, making strong relationships, exercising his right to move freely at will and 'communicating' with those around him. His communication, although very limited, is quite effective with those who know him. The next piece of the jigsaw is to provide Gavin with the tools for speech so that he will be able to extend his dialogue to a wider arena, thereby taking a little more control of the way he conducts his life.

After all, isn't this what we all do?

References

References to Foreword

Brinker, R.P. (1978) Teaching language in context, a feasibility study. *Revue de Phonétique Appliquée*, 46-7, 195-208.

Donaldson, M. (1978) *Children's Minds* (London: Fontana).

Freire, P. (1973) *Pedagogy of the Oppressed* (New York: Seabury).

Gibbs, G. (1992) *Improving the Quality of Student Learning* (Bristol: Technical and Educational Services).

References to Chapter One

Ashman, A.F. (1985) Problem solving and planning: two sides of the same coin. In Ashman, A.F. and Laura, R.S. (Eds.) *The Education and Training of the Mentally Retarded* (London: Croom Helm).

Ashman, A. and Conway, R. (1989) *Cognitive Strategies for Special Education* (London: Routledge).

Belmont, J.M. (1978) Individual differences in memory: The causes of normal and retarded development. In Gruneberg, M. and Morris, P. (Eds.) *Aspects of Memory* (London: Methuen).

Borkowski, J.G. and Cavanagh, J. (1979) Maintenance and generalisation of skills and strategies by the retarded. In Ellis, N.R. (Ed.) *Handbook of Mental Deficiency; Psychological Theory and Research* (Hillsdale, NJ: Erlbaum).

Borkowski, J.G. and Konarski, E.A. (1981) Educational implications of efforts to train intelligence. *The Journal of Special Education*, 15(2), 289–305.

Brinker, R.P. and Lewis, M. (1982) Discovering the competent handi-capped infant. In Process Approach to Assessment and Intervention, *Topics in Early Childhood*, 2, 1–16

Brown, A.L. (1974) The role of strategic behaviour in retardate memory. In Ellis, N.R. (Ed.) *International Review of Research in Mental Retardation* Vol. 1 (New York: Academic Press).

Brown, A.L. (1978) Knowing when, where and how to remember: A problem of metacognition. In Glaser R. (Ed.) *Advances in Instructional Psychology* (Hillsdale, NJ: Erlbaum)

Brown, A.L. and Campione, J.C. (1986) Psychological theory and the study of learning disabilities. *American Psychologist*, 14(10), 1059–1068.

Bruner, J. (1978) The role of dialogue in language acquisition. In Sinclair, A., Jarvella, R.J. and Levelt, W.J.M. (Eds.) *The Child's Conception of Language* (Berlin, West Germany: Springer-Verlag).

Burden, R. (1991) Underpinning the curriculum: the development of cognitive skills and strategies. In Smith, B. (Ed.) *Interactive Approaches to Teaching the Core Curriculum* (Birmingham: Newman-Westhill Colleges).

Butterfield, E.C., Wambold, C. and Belmont, J.M. (1973) On the theory and practice of improving short-term memory. *American Journal of Mental Deficiency*, 77, 654–669.

Campione, J.N. and Brown, A.L. (1978) Toward a theory of intelligence: Contributions from research with retarded children. *Intelligence* 2, 279–304.

Dearden, R.F. (1968) *The Philosophy of Primary Education* (London: Routledge and Kegan Paul).

Feuerstein, R., Rand, Y., Hoffman, M.B. and Miller, R. (1980) *Instrumental Enrichment: an Intervention Programme for Cognition Modifiability* (Baltimore: University Park Press).

Feuerstein, R., Rand, Y.E. and Rynders, J.E. (1988) *Don 't Accept Me as I am!* (New York: Plenum Press).

Flavell, J.H. (1976) Metacognitive aspects of problem solving. In Resnick, L.B. (Ed.) *The Nature of Intelligence* (Hillsdale, NJ: Erlbaum).

Glaser, R. (1984) Education and thinking. *American Psychologist*, 39, 93–104.

Glenn, S. (1988) Interactive approaches to working with children with profound and multiple learning difficulties. In Smith, B. (Ed.) *Interactive Approaches to the Education of Children with Severe Learning Difficulties* (Birmingham: Westhill College).

Glidden, L.R. (1979) Training of learning and memory in retarded persons: strategies, techniques, and teaching tools. In Ellis (Ed.) *Handbook of Mental Deficiency; Psychological Theory and Research* (Hillsdale, NJ: Erlbaum).

Greenfield, P.M. (1984) A theory of the teacher in the learning activities of everyday life. In Rogoff, B. and Lave, J. (Eds.) *Everyday Cognition: Its Development in Social Context* (Cambridge, Mass.: Harvard University Press).

152

Hewitt, D. and Nind, M. (1988) Developing an interactive curriculum for pupils with severe and complex learning difficulties. A classroom process. In Smith, B. (Ed.) *Interactive Approaches to the Education of Children with Severe Learning Difficulties* (Birmingham: Westhill College).

Homer, R.H., Dunlap, G., and Koegel, R.L. (Eds.), *Generalisation and Maintenance* (Baltimore: Brookes).

Kiernan, C. and Woodford, F. (Eds.) (1975) *Behaviour Modification with the Severely Retarded* (Amsterdam: IRMH Study Group 8, Associated Scientific Publishers).

Litrownik, A.J. (1978) *Self-concept and self-regulatory processes in TMRs* (Final Report, Grant No GP 75-06670) (Bureau of Education for the Handicapped, U.S. Office of Health, Education and Welfare).

Maier, S.F. and Seligman, M.E.P. (1976) Learned helplessness: theory and evidence. *Journal of Experimental Psychology*, 105, 3–46.

McConkey, R. (1981) Education without understanding? *Special Education; Forward Trends*, 8(3), 8–10.

Miller, G.A., Galanter, E., and Pribram, K.H. (1960) *Plans and Structures of Behaviour* (New York: Holt).

Newson, J. (1979) The growth of shared understanding between infant and caregiver. In Bullowa, M. (Ed.) *Before Speech* (Cambridge University Press).

Piaget, J. (1950) *The Psychology of Intelligence* (New York: Harcourt Brace).

Potts, W.A. (1911) *The Official Reports of the Poor Law Conferences 1911–1912* (London: Central Committee of Poor Law Conferences).

Punukollu, N.R. (1991) *How to Develop Comprehensive Community Mental Handicap Services* (International Institute of Crisis Intervention).

Ross, D.M. and Ross, S.A. (1978) *Pacemaker Primary Curriculum* (Belmont, California: Fearon).

Schaffer, H.R. (1977) Early interactive development. In Schaffer, H.R. (Ed.) *Studies in Mother – Infant Interaction* (New York: Academic Press).

Schwieso, J.J., Hastings, N.J. and Stainthorp, R. (1992) Psychology in Teacher Education: A response to Tomlinson. *The Psychologist,* 5 (3), 112–113.

Shapiro, E.S. (1981) Self-control procedures with the mentally retarded. In Mittersen, R.M., Eisler, and Miller, P.M. (Eds.) *Progress in Behavior Modification* (New York: Academic Press).

Staff of Rectory Paddock School (1983) *In Search of a Curriculum (2nd edn.)* (Sidcup, Kent: Robin Wren Publications).

Stephens, B. (1977) A Piagetian approach to curriculum development for the severely, profoundly and multiply handicapped. In Sontag, E. Smith, J. and Certo, N. (Eds.) *Educational Programming for the Severely and Profoundly Handicapped* (USA: Division on Mental Retardation, The Council for Exceptional Children).

Vygotsky, L.S. (1978) *Mind and Society.* In Cole, M., John-Steiner, V,. Scribner, S. and Souberman, E. (Eds.) (Cambridge, Mass.: Harvard University Press).

Vygotsky, L.S. (1962) *Thought and Language* (Cambridge, Mass.: MIT Press).

Watson, J. and Knight, C. (1991) An evaluation of intensive interactive teaching with pupils with very severe learning difficulties *Child Language Teaching and Therapy,* 7(3), 310–325

Wertsch, J.V. (1978) Adult-child interaction and the roots of metacognition. *Quarterly Newsletter of the Institute for Comparative Human Development,* 1, 15–18.

Whitman, T. (1990) Self-regulation and mental retardation. *American Journal on Mental Retardation,* 94(4), 347–362.

Wood, D., Bruner, J.S. and Ross, G. *(1976)* The role of tutoring in problem solving. *Journal of Child Psychology and Psychiatry,* 17, 89–100.

Wood, S. and Shears, B. *(1986) Teaching Children with Severe Learning Difficulties*; *A radical reappraisal* (London: Croom Helm).

References to Chapter Two

Ainscow, M. and Tweddle, D. (1988) *Encouraging Classroom Success* (London: Fulton).

Baker, P.A. (1991) The denial of adolescence for people with mental handicaps : An Unwitting Conspiracy? *Mental Handicap,* 19 (2), 61–65.

Bank-Mikkelsen, N.E. (1969) A metropolitan area in Denmark: Copenhagen. In Kugel, R.B. and Wolfensberger, W.P. (Eds.) *Changing Patterns in Residential Services for the Mentally Retarded* (Washington).

Bannerman, D.J., Sheldon, J.B., Sherman, J.A. and Harchik, A.E. (1990) Balancing the right to habilitation with the right to personal liberties: The rights of people with developmental disabilities to eat too many doughnuts and take a nap. *Journal of Applied Behaviour Analysis,* 23 (1), 79–89.

Brechin, A. and Swain, J. (1989) Creating a 'Working Alliance' with people with learning difficulties. In Brechin, A. and Walmsley, J. (Eds.) *Making Connections : Reflecting on the Lives and Experiences of People with Learning Difficulties* (London: Hodder & Stoughton).

Brisenden, S. (1986) Independent living and the medical model. *Disability Handicap and Society,* 1 (2), 173–178.

Carr, E.G. and Durand, V.M. (1985) Reducing behaviour problems through functional communication training. *Journal of Applied Behaviour Analysis,* 18, 111–126.

Chappell, A.L. (1992) Towards a sociological critique of the normalisation principle. *Disability, Handicap & Society,* 7, (1) 35–51.

154

DES (1978) *Special Educational Needs: Report of the Committee of Enquiry into the Education of Handicapped Children and Young People* (London: HMSO).

DES (1988) *The Education Reform Act, 1988.* (London: HMSO).

Durand, V.M. and Crimmins, D. (1991) Teaching functionally equivalent responses as an intervention for challenging behaviour. In Remington, B. (Ed.) *The Challenge of Severe Mental Handicap : A Behaviour Analytic Approach* (London: Wiley).

Dyer, K., Dunlap, G., and Winterling, V. (1990) Effects of choice making on the serious problem behaviours of students with severe handicaps. *Journal of Applied Behaviour Analysis*, 23 (4), 515–524.

Further Education Unit (1992) *Supporting Transition to Adulthood* (Wigwam Pub. Services).

Gardner, J., Murphy, J. and Crawford, N. (1983). *The Skills Analysis Model* (Kidderminster: BIMH).

Guess, D., Benson, H.A. and Siegal-Causey, E. (1985) Concepts and issues related to choice making and autonomy among persons with severe disabilities. *Journal of the Association for Persons with Severe Handicaps* 10 (2), 79–86.

Houghton, J., Bronicki, G. and Guess, D. (1987) Opportunities to express preferences and make choices among students with severe disabilities in classroom settings. *Journal of the Association for Persons with Severe Handicaps*, 12 (1), 18–27.

Hughes, J.M. (1975) The educational needs of the mentally handicapped. *Educational Research*, 17 (3), 228–233.

Kiernan, C. (1991) Research : Progress and prospects. In Segal, S.S. and Varma, V.P. (Eds.) *Prospects for People with Learning Difficulties* (London: David Fulton).

Koegal, R.L., Dyer, K. and Bell, L.K. (1987) The Influence of child-preferred activities on autistic children's social behaviour. *Journal of Applied Behaviour Analysis*, 20 (3), 243–252.

Leeming, K., Swann, W., Coupe J. and Mittler P. (1979) *Teaching Language and Communication to the Mentally Handicapped* (London : Methuen).

Melland School (1993) *Cross Curricular Elements: Themes, Skills and Dimensions* Curriculum Document.

Meyer, L.H. (1991) Guest editorial – Why Meaningful Outcomes? *The Journal of Special Education*, 25 (3), 287–290.

Monty, R.A., Geller, E.S., Savage, R.E. and Perlmuter, L.C. (1979) The freedom to choose is not always so choice. *Journal of Experimental Psychology: Human Learning and Memory*, 5 (2),170–178.

National Curriculum Council (1990) *Curriculum Guidelines 3.*

155

Oliver, M. (1989) Disability and dependency: a creation of industrial societies? In Barton, L. (Ed.) *Disability and Dependency* (London: Falmer).

Oliver, C. (1991) The application of analogue methodology to the functional analysis of challenging behaviour. In Remington, B. (Ed.) *The Challenge of Severe Mental Handicap: A Behaviour Analytic Approach* (London: Wiley).

Parsons, M.B. and Reid, D.H. (1990) Assessing food preferences among people with profound mental retardation: Providing opportunities to make choices. *Journal of Applied Behaviour Analysis*, 23 (2), 183–195.

Parsons, M.B., Reid, D.H., Reynolds, J. and Bumgarner, M. (1990) Effects of chosen versus assigned jobs on the work performance of persons with severe handicaps. *Journal of Applied Behaviour Analysis*, 23 (2), 253–258.

Realon, R.E., Favell, J.E. and Lowerre, A. (1990) The effects of making choices on engagement levels with persons who are profoundly multiply handicapped. *Education and Training in Mental Retardation*, 25, 299–305.

Rincover, A., Newson, C.D., Lovaas, O.I. and Koegal, R.L. (1977) Some motivational properties of sensory stimulation in psychotic children. *Journal of Experimental Child Psychology*, 24, 312–323.

Rincover, A., Cook, R., Peoples, A. and Packard, D. (1979) Sensory extinction and sensory reinforcement principles for programming multiple adaptive behaviour change. *Journal of Applied Behaviour Analysis*, 12 (2), 221–233.

Shevin, M. and Klein, N.K. (1984) The importance of choice making skills for students with severe learning disabilities. *Journal of the Association for Persons with Severe Handicaps*, 9 (3), 159–166.

Simpson, P.F. (1967) Training Centres – A Challenge. *Special Education*, 56, 34–38.

Bibliography

Manchester City Council Education Department *Implementing the Whole Curriculum. Cross Curricular Themes. Skills. Dimensions* (1991).

Manchester City Council Education Department *Implementing the Whole Curriculum. Cross Curricular Themes. Citizenship* (1991).

Manchester City Council Education Department *Implementing the Whole Curriculum. Cross Curricular Themes. Environmental Education* (1991).

Manchester City Council Education Department *Implementing the Whole Curriculum. Cross Curricular Themes. Economic and Industrial Awareness* (1991).

Manchester City Council Education Department *Implementing the Whole Curriculum. Cross Curricular Themes. Health Education* (1991).
Manchester City Council Education Department *Implementing the Whole Curriculum. Cross Curricular Themes. Careers* (1991).

References to Chapter Three

Astington, J.W. and Gopnik, A. (1991) Theoretical explanations of children's understanding of the mind. *British Journal of Developmental Psychology*, 9, 1, 7–31.

Bremmer, J.G. (1988) *Infancy* (Oxford: Blackwell).

Bruner, J.S. and Sherwood, V. (1976) Early rule structure: the case of peekaboo. In Bruner, J.S., Jolly, A. and Sylva, K. (Eds.) *Play: Its Role in Evolution and Development* (Harmondsworth: Penguin).

Byatt, A.S. (1990) *Possession: A Romance* (London: Chatto and Windus).

Dore, J. (1974) A pragmatic description of early language development. *Journal of Psycholinguistic Research*, 4, 343–350.

Dore, J. (1977) Children's illocutionary acts. In R.O. Freedle (Ed.) *Discourse, Production and Comprehension* (Norwood, New Jersey: Ablex Publishing Corporation).

Durand, V.M. (1990) *Functional Communication Training: an intervention programme for severe behaviour problems* (Hove: Guilford Press).

Hymes, D. (1971) Competence and performance in linguistic theory. In R. Huxley and D. Ingram (Eds.) *Language Acquisition: Models and Methods* (London: Academic Press).

Luria, A.R. (1959) The directive function of speech in development and dissolution, Part 1, No.3. Reprinted in R.C. Oldfield and J.C. Marshall (Eds.) *Language: Selected Readings* (Harmondsworth: Penguin).

McGee, J.J., Menolascino, F.J., Hobbs, D.C. and Menousek, P.E. (1987) *Gentle Teaching: a non-aversive approach to helping persons with mental retardation* (New York: Human Sciences Press).

Meade, G.H. (1934) *Mind, Self and Society* (Chicago: University of Chicago Press).

Piaget, J. and Inhelder, B. (1969) *The Psychology of the Child* (London: Routledge and Kegan Paul).

Schaffer, H.R. (1971) *The Growth of Sociability* (Harmondsworth: Penguin).

Schaffer, H.R. (1977) *Studies in Mother Infant Interaction* (London: Academic Press).

Searle, J.R. (1969) *Speech Acts: An Essay on the Philosophy of Language* (Cambridge: Cambridge Univeristy Press).

Shotter, J. (1973) Acquired powers. the transformation of natural into personal powers. *Journal for the Theory of Social Behaviour*, 3, 2, 141–156.

Vygotsky, L.S. (1978) *Mind in Society: The Development of Higher Psychological Processes* (Cambridge, Mass: Harvard University Press).

References to Chapter Four (a)

Bell, P.B. (1980) *Characteristics of handicapped infants: A study of the relationship between child characteristics and stress as reported by Mother* (Unpublished doctoral dissertation, N.Carolina, USA).

Berger, J. and Cunningham, C. (1983) Development of early vocal behaviours and interactions in Down's Syndrome and non-handicapped infant-mother pairs. *Developmental Psychology* 19, 322–331.

Blacher, J. (1984) A dynamic perspective on the impact of a severely handicapped child on the family. In Blacher, J. (Ed.) *Severely Handicapped Young Children and their Families* (Academic Press).

Brinker, R.P. and Lewis, M. (1982) Discovering the competent handicapped infant. In Process Approach to Assessment and Intervention. *Topics in Early Childhood* 2, 1–16.

Buckhalt, J., Rutherford, R and Goldberg, K. (1987) Verbal and non-verbal intervention of mothers with their Down's Syndrome and non-retarded infants. *American Journal of Mental Deficiency*, 79, 52–58.

Coupe, J., Barton, L., Barber, M., Levy, D,. Murphy D. and Collins, L. (1985) *Affective Communication Assessment* (Manchester: Manchester Education Committee).

Emde, R.N. and Brown, C. (1978) Adaptation to the birth of a Down's Syndrome Infant: Grieving and maternal attachment. *Journal of American Academic Child Psychology*, 17, 299–323.

Glenn, S. (1986) *Interactive approaches to work with children with profound and multiple learning difficulties* (Unpublished paper, Lancashire Polytechnic).

Glenn, S.M. and Cunningham, C.C. (1982) Recognition of the familiar words of nursery rhymes by handicapped and non-handicapped infants. *Journal of Child Psychology and Psychiatry*, 23, 319–327.

Glenn, S.M. and Cunningham, C.C. (1983) What do babies listen to most? *Developmental Psychology*, 19, 332–337.

Glenn, S.M. and Cunningham, C.C. (1984a) Selective preferences to different speech stimuli in infants with Down's Syndrome. In Berk, K. (Ed.) *Perspectives and Progress in Mental Retardation Vol. 1* (Baltimore: University Park Press).

Glenn, S.M. and Cunningham, C.C. (1984b) The use of nursery rhymes in early language learning with prelinguistic mentally handicapped children. *Exceptional Children* 51, 72–74.

158

Hartka, E. and Lewis, M. (1981) *Age changes in contingent learning.* Paper presented at the annual meeting of the Educational Psychological Association, New York, USA.

Jones, O.M. (1980) Prelinguistic communication skills in Down's Syndrome and normal infants. In Field, T. (Ed.) *High Risk Infants and Children: Adult and Parent Interactions* (New York: Academic Press).

Khan, J.V. (1976) Utility of the Uzgiris and Hunt Scales of sensory motor development with severely and profoundly retarded children. *American Journal of Mental Deficiency,* 80, 663–665.

Lewis, M. and Goldberg, S. (1969) Perceptual-cognitive development in infancy: A generalised expectancy model as a function of mother infant interaction. *Merril-Palmer Quarterly,* 15, 81–100.

Lewis, M. and Rosenblum, L. (1974) *The Effect of the Infant on its Caregiver: The Origins of Behaviour Vol. 1* (New York: Wiley).

Lewis, M., Sullivan, M.W. and Brooks-Gunn, J. (1985) Emotional behaviour during the learning of a contingency in early infancy. *British Journal of Developmental Psychology,* 3, 307–316.

Lewis, M. and Wehren, A. (1982) The tyranny of the central tendency and other problems in studying the handicapped child. In Brinker, D. (Ed.) *Application of Research Findings to Intervention with At-Risk and Handicapped Infants* (Baltimore: University Park Press).

Lovett, S. (1985) Micro electronic and computer based technology. In Clarke, A.M., Clarke, A.D.B. and Berg, J. (Eds.) *Mental Deficiency: the Changing Outlook* (London: Methuen).

MacPherson, F.D. and Butterworth, G.E. (1981) *Application of a Piagetian infant developmental scale to the assessment of profoundly mentally handicapped children.* Paper presented to the Annual Conference: Developmental Psychology Section. British Psychological Society. Manchester U.K.

Millar, W.S. (1972) A study of Operant Conditioning under Delayed Reinforcement in early infancy. *Monographs of the Society of Research in Child Development,* 37, (2 serial 147).

Piaget, J. (1952) *The Origins of Intelligence in Children* (New York: International University Press).

Rice, H.K., McDaniels, M.W., Stallings, V.D. and Gatz, M.J. (1967) Operant Conditioning in Vegetable Patients. *Psychological Record,* 17, 449–460.

Rogers, S. J. (1977) Characteristics of cognitive development of profoundly retarded children. *Child Development* 48, 837–843.

Seligman, M. (1975) *Helplessness: On Depression, Development and Death* (San Francisco: Freeman).

Snyder-McLean, B.S., McLean, J.E. and Sack, S. (1984) Structuring Joint Action Routines: A Strategy for Facilitating Communication and Language Development in the Classroom. *Seminars in Speech and Language*, 5, 3.

Vygotsky, L.S. (1978) *Mind in Society: The Development of the Higher Psychological Processes* (Cambridge: Harvard University Press).

Watson, J. (1966) The development and generalisation of 'contingency awareness' in early infancy: some hypotheses. *Merril-Palmer Quarterly*, 14, 123–135.

Watson, J. (1967) Memory and contingency analysis in infant learning. *Merril-Palmer Quarterly*, 13, 55–76.

Watson, J. and Ramey, C.T. (1972) Reactions to response-contingency stimulation in early infancy. *Merril-Palmer Quarterly*, 18, 219–227.

Woodward, M. (1959) The behaviour of idiots interpreted by Piaget's theory of sensori-motor development. *British Journal of Educational Psychology*, 29, 60–71.

References to Chapter Four (b)

Bruner, J. and Connolly, K. (1974) *The Growth of Competence* (London: Academic Press).

Clare, M. (1990) *Developing Self-Advocacy Skills with People with Disabilities and Learning Difficulties* (London: F.E.U.).

Davis, M. (1985) *The Usefulness of an Interactive Approach to the Education of Severely and Profoundly Handicapped Individuals* (Unpublished dissertation, Herefordshire College of Further Education).

Day, C., Whitaker, P. and Wren, D. (1987) *Appraisal and Professional Development in Primary Schools* (Milton Keynes: Open University Press).

Eisner, E.W. (1969) Instructional and expressive objectives: their formulation and use in the curriculum. In Popham, W.J. *et al.* (Eds.) *Objectives and Instruction* (London: Routledge and Kegan Paul).

Finch, J. (1984) *Education and Social Policy* (London: Longman).

Fraser, B. (1984) *Society, Schools and Handicap* (Cheshire: NCSE).

Kelly, A.V. (1972) *The Curriculum: Theory and Practice* (London: Paul Chapman).

McConkey, R. (1981) Education without understanding? *Special Education: Forward Trends*, 8 (3).

McGee, J.J., Menolascino, F.J., Hobbs, D.C. and Menousek, P.E. (1987) *Gentle Teaching: a Non-Aversive Approach to Helping Persons with Mental Retardation* (New York: Human Sciences Press).

Tomlinson, S. and Barton, L. (1987) *A Sociological Perspective in Special Education: Policy, Practices and Social Issues* (Bath: Pitman Press).

Upton, G. and Cooper, P. (1990) Perspectives on Behaviour Problems in Schools: The Ecosystemic Approach. *Journal of Therapeutic Education*, 9 (1).

Wood, S. and Shears, B. (1986) *Teaching Children with Severe Learning Difficulties: A Radical Re-appraisal* (Beckenham: Croom Helm).

References to Chapter Five

Ashman, A.F. and Conway, R.N.F. (1989) *Cognitive Strategies for Special Education* (London: Taylor and Francis).

Brown, M. (1991) *The High/Scope Approach to the National Curriculum Book 1: An Introduction* (London: High/Scope UK).

Dennison, B. and Kirk, R. (1990) *Do, Review, Learn, Apply: A Simple Guide To Experiential Learning* (Oxford: Basil Blackwell).

DES (1978) *Special Educational Needs* (The Warnock Report) (London: HMSO).

Dewey, J. (1964a) My Pedagogic Creed. In Archamault, R.D. (Ed.) *John Dewey on Education, Selected Writings* (Chicago: University of Chicago Press).

Dewey, J. (1964b) The Child and the Curriculum. In Archamault, R.D. (Ed.) *John Dewey on Education, Selected Writings* (Chicago: University of Chicago Press).

High Scope K–3 Curriculum Guide Series (1991) (Michigan, USA: The High/Scope Press).

Hohmann, M., Banet, B. and Weikart, D.P. (1979) *Young Children in Action* (Michigan: The High/Scope Press).

Jordon, R. and Powell, S (1990) High/Scope – A Cautionary View. *Early Years*, 11, (1) 29–33.

Knight, C. (1991) Developing Communication Through Interaction. In Watson, J. (Ed.) *Innovatory Practice & Severe Learning Difficulties* (Edinburgh: Moray House Publications).

Longhorn, F. (1988) *A Sensory Curriculum For Very Special People* (London: Souvenir Press, Human Horizon Series).

Mc Conkey, R (1987) Interaction: The Name Of The Game. In: Smith, B. (1987) (Ed.) *Interactive Approaches to the Education of Children with Severe Learning Difficulties* (Birmingham: Westhill College).

Piaget, J. (1970) Piaget's Theory. In Mussen, P. (Ed.) *Carmichael's Manual of Child Psychology* 3rd edition, Vol. 1 (New York: Wiley).

Schweinhart, L. (1988) *A School Adminstrator's Guide to Early Childhood Programs* (Michigan: The High/Scope Press).

Skinner, B.F. (1968) *The Technology of Teaching* (New York: Appleton-Century Crofts).

Smilansky, S. (1968) *The Effects of Sociodramatic Play on Disadvantaged Pre School Children* (New York: John Wiley).

Smith, B. (1989) Which Approach? The Education of Children With Severe Learning Difficulties. *Mental Handicap*, 17 (3), 111–115.

Smith, B. (1991) (Ed.) *Interactive Approaches to Teaching the Core Subjects: The National Curriculum for Pupils with Severe and Moderate Learning Difficulties* (Bristol: Lame Duck Publications).

Tomlinson, P.D. (1989) The Teaching of Skill : Modern cognitive perspective. In Sugden, D. (1989) (Ed.) *Cognitive Approaches in Special Education* (London: Falmer Press).

Tompkins, M. (1991) 'Special' Children: Building on their strengths. In Brickman, N.A. and Taylor, L.S. (Eds.) *Supporting Young Learners: Ideas For Pre School And Day Care Providers* (Michigan: The High/Scope Press).

Vygotsky, L.S. (1962) *Thought and Language* (New York: Wiley).

Warwickshire County Council (1989)*The National Curriculum. Key Experiences and the Learning of Young Children* (Warwickshire County Council).

Weikart, D.P. (1989) The High/Scope Curriculum in Practice. In *The High/Scope Project: Perspectives 40* (University of Exeter: School of Education).

References to Chapter Six

Alexander, R., Rose,J. and Woodhead,C. (1992) *Curriculum Organisation and Classroom Practice in Primary Schools* (London: HMSO).

Ashdown, R., Carpenter, B. and Bovair, K. (Eds.) (1991) *The Curriculum Challenge: Access to the National Curriculum for Pupils with Learning Difficulties* (London: Falmer).

Byers, R. (1992) Topics: from myths to objectives. In Upton, G. Bovair, K. and Carpenter, B. (Eds.) *Special Curriculum Needs* (London: Fulton).

DES (1989) *English in the National Curriculum* (London: HMSO).

DES (1990) *Technology in the National Curriculum* (London: HMSO).

DES (1991a) *Geography in the National Curriculum* (London: HMSO).

DES (1991b) *History in the National Curriculum* (London: HMSO).

DES (1991c) *Mathematics in the National Curriculum* (London: HMSO).

DES (1991d) *Science in the National Curriculum* (London: HMSO).

Friere P. (1972) *Pedagogy of the Oppressed* (Harmondsworth: Penguin Books).

McGee, J.J., Menolascino, F.J., Hobbs, D.C. and Menousek, P.E. (1987) *Gentle Teaching – a Non-aversive Approach to Helping Persons with Mental Retardation* (New York: Human Sciences Press).

162

NCC (1989) *Mathematics: Non-Statutory Guidance* (York: NCC).

NCC (1990a) *Curriculum Guidance 3 – The Whole Curriculum* (York: NCC).

NCC (1990b) *Information Technology: Non-Statutory Guidance* (York: NCC).

NCC (1990c) *Curriculum Guidance 4 – Education for Economic and Industrial Understanding* (York: NCC).

NCC (1992) Curriculum Guidance 9 – *The National Curriculum and Pupils with Severe Learning Difficulties* (York: NCC).

Nind, M. and Hewitt, D. (1988) Interaction as Curriculum *British Journal of Special Education*, 15 (2), 55–57.

Sebba, J. and Byers, R. (1992) The National Curriculum: Control or Liberation for Pupils with Learning Difficulties. *The Curriculum Journal*, 3 (1).

Sebba, J., Byers, R. and Rose, R. (1993) *Redefining the Whole Curriculum for Pupils with Learning Difficulties* (London: Fulton).

Smith B. (Ed.) (1988) *Interactive Approaches to the Education of Children with Severe Learning Difficulties* (Birmingham: Westhill College).

References to Chapter Seven

Ashdown, R., Carpenter, B. and Bovair K. (1991) The Curriculum Challenge. In Ashdown, R., Carpenter B. and Bovair K. (Eds.) *The Curriculum Challenge* (London: Falmer Press).

Birmingham City Council Education Department (1990) *The TVE Entitlements* (Birmingham: Education Department).

Bovair, K. (1990) Special Educators – Special Education: THIS ISN'T KANSAS TOTO? In Baker, D. and Bovair. K. (Eds.) *Making the Special Schools Ordinary Vol. 2* (London: Falmer Press).

Broadfoot, P., James M., McMeeking, S., Nuttall, D. and Stierer, B. (1988) *Records of Achievement: Record of the National Evaluation of Pilot Schemes* (London: HMSO).

Broadfoot P., Grant, M., James, M., Nuttall, D. and Stierer, B. (1991) *Records of Achievement. Report of the National Evaluation of Extension Work in Pilot Schemes* (London: HMSO).

Carpenter, B. and Lewis, A. (1989) Searching for Solutions: Approaches to Planning the Curriculum for Integration of SLD and PSLD Children. In Baker D. and Bovair, K. (Eds.) *Making The Special Schools Ordinary* (London: Falmer Press).

Cassell, B., Lindoe, S. and Skilling, C. (1991) TVEI and its relationship to the National Curriculum. In Ashdown, R., Carpenter, B. and Bovair K. (Eds.) *The Curriculum Challenge* (London: Falmer Press).

Cohen, R. and Bradley R. (1978) Simulation games, learning and retention. *Elementary School Journal*, 78, 247–253.

Conquest, M., Pirt, G and Wright, M. (1990) Recording the achievement of pupils. In Baker, D. and Bovair, K. (Eds.) *Making The Special Schools Ordinary Vol. 2* (London: Falmer Press).

Cooper, D. (1987) TVEI: Across the Ability Range? *British Journal of Special Education*, 14 (4), 147–149.

DES and the Welsh Office (1984) *Records of Achievement: A Statement of Policy* (London: HMSO).

DES and the Welsh Office (1989) *Report of the Records of Achievement Steering Committee* (London: HMSO).

DES and Welsh Office (1991) *Technical and Vocational Education Initiative (TVEI) England and Wales 1983–90* (London: HMSO).

Employment Department Group (1992) *TVEI: A Study of The Impact of TVEI on Young People with Special Educational Needs* (London: Social And Community Planning Research). Copies obtainable from TVEI Enquiry Point, Meads, P.O Box 12, Nottingham NG7 4GB.

Fagg, S. (1991) Perspectives on the National Curriculum. In Ashdown, R., Carpenter, B. and Bovair, K. (Eds.) *The Curriculum Challenge* (London: Falmer Press).

Galletley, I. (1989) A new curriculum for the later years. In Baker, D. and Bovair, K. (Eds.) *Making The Special Schools Ordinary* (London: Falmer Press).

The London Record of Achievement (1989) *Putting Students First* (London: ILEA).

Midlands TVEI Special Needs Group (1991) *A digest of interesting practice* No 4 (c/o Liz Hayes, EIC, Solihull B36 ONF).

Moseley School (1991) *Appendix 6 Schools Curriculum Award Submission 1991* (Birmingham: Moseley School).

Peter, M. (1987) Whose Initiatives? *British Journal of Special Education*, 14 (4), 136.

Smith, B. (1988) *Interactive Approaches to the Education of Children with Severe Learning Difficulties* (Birmingham: Westhill College).

Smith, B. (1991) Introduction and background to Interactive Approaches. In Smith, B. (Ed.) *Interactive Approaches to Teaching the Core Subjects* (Bristol: Lame Duck).

The Training Agency, TVEI AI (1989a) *Curricular Changes 1982–1987* (London: The Training Agency).

The Training Agency, TVEI R14 (1989b) *TVEI Special Education Needs Directory* (London: The Training Agency).

The Training Agency, Com. L7 (1989c) *Compacts* (Sheffield: The Training Agency).

Wedell, K. (1988) The new Act: A special need for vigilance. *British Journal of Special Education*, 15 (3), 98–101.

164

West Midlands Monitoring Group (SLD) (1991) *Broadsheet No 5* (West Midlands: National Curriculum Monitoring Group – SLD)

Wolfendale. S. (1989) Making Education Accessible: Parents' Role in Special Needs Provision. In Baker, D. and Bovair, K (Eds.) *Making the Special Schools Ordinary* Vol. 1 (London: Falmer Press).

References to Chapter Eight

Boulton, A. (1988) Decision making for students with severe learning difficulties in further education context. *Educare* 30, 15–20.

Brandon, D. (1988) Self advocacy—more head patting than listening. *Community Living, 2 (2)*.

Clare, M. (1990) *Developing Self Advocacy Skills With People With Disabilities and Learning Difficulties* (London:FEU).

Deacon, J. (1974) *Tongue Tied* (NSMHC)

Dumbleton, P. (1990) A philosophy of education for all. *British Journal of Education,* 17(1), 16–18.

Flynn, M. and Ward, L. (1991) We can change the future. In Segal, S. and Varma, V. (Eds.) *Prospects for People with Learning Difficulties* (London: Fulton).

Hewlett, M. (1986) *Curriculum to Serve Society. How Schools Work For People* (Loughborough: Newstead Publ.).

Johnstone, D. (1988) Curricular considerations since Warnock: Towards a negotiated standing. *Vocational Aspect of Education* 107 (XL), 111–115.

Lindsay, A. and Marlen, R. (1989) Unrealistic Expectations. *Nursing Times,* 85 (42), 33–34.

NCC (1990) *Education For Citizenship.* (York: NCC).

Wertheimer,A. (1989) *Self Advocacy and Parents: The impact of self-advocacy on the parents of young people with disabilities* (London: FEU).

Whelan, E. and Speake, B.(1981) *Getting to Work* (London: Souvenir Press).

Whittaker, A. (1988) A voice of their own. *The Newsletter of the Kings Fund* 11 (4), 1–2.

Williams, P. and Shoultz B. (1982) *We Can Speak For Ourselves* (London: Souvenir Press).

Wolfensberger, W. (1972) *The Principle of Normalisation In Human Services* (Toronto: National Institute of Mental Retardation).

References to Chapter Nine

Atkinson, D. (1987) How easy is it for friendship? *Social Work Today,* 15, 12–13

Bailey, R., Matthews F., and Leckie, C. (1986) Feeling – the way ahead in mental handicap. *Mental Handicap*, 14, 65–67.

Bees, S. (1991) Some aspects of the friendship networks of people with learning difficulties. *Clinical Psychology Forum*, 31, 12–14.

Campaign for Mentally Handicapped People (1972) *Our Life* (London: CMH).

Cattermole, M., Jahoda, A, and Markova, I. (1988) Life in a mental handicap hospital: the view from the inside. *Mental Handicap*, 16, 136–139.

Crawley, B. (1982) *The Feasibility of Trainee Committees as a means of Self Advocacy in Adult Training Centres in England and Wales.* (Unpublished PhD thesis, Manchester).

Evans, H. (1987) Antur Waunfawr (the 'Waunfawr Venture') ii: Its early development and achievements. *Mental Handicap*, 15, 108–111.

Flynn, M. and Ward, L. (1991) 'We can change the future': Self citizen advocacy. In Segal, S. and Varma, V. (Eds.) *Prospects for People with Learning Difficulties* (London: Fulton).

Jeffree, D. and Cheseldine, S. (1980) *Junior Interest Profile* (Manchester: Hester Adrian Research Centre).

John, P. and Eaton, D. (1991) *Risk Taking Policy* (Unpublished report, Manchester: South Manchester Joint Services for People with Learning Difficulties).

Lindsay, W. and Baty, F. (1986) Abbreviated progressive relaxation: its use with adults who are mentally handicapped. *Mental Handicap*, 14, 123–126.

Lindsay, W. and Kasprowicz, M. (1987) Challenging negative cognitions: developing confidence in adults by means of cognitive behaviour therapy. *Mental Handicap*, 15, 159–162.

North Western Regional Health Authority (1982) *Services for People who are mentally handicapped: a model district service* (Manchester: NWRHA).

Novaco, R. (1985) Anger control therapy. In Bellack, A. and Hersen, M. (Eds.) *Dictionary of Behaviour Therapy Techniques* (New York: Pergamon Press).

O'Brien, J. and Tyne, A. (1981) *The Principle of Normalisation: A Foundation for Effective Services* (London: Campaign for the Mentally Handicapped).

Raynes, N. (1991) Obstacles to community care. In Segal, S. and Varma, V. (Eds.) *Prospects for People with Learning Difficulties* (London: Fulton).

Simons, K., Booth, T. and Booth, W. (1991) Speaking Out: user studies and people with learning difficulties. *Research, Policy and Planning*, 7, 9–17.

166

South Manchester Brindle Lodge Group (1991) *Time for Talking* (Oldham: Northwest SEMFRC).

Speake, B. (1978) *The Effectiveness of Work Preparation Courses for Educationally Disadvantaged School Leavers.* (Unpublished PhD thesis, Manchester).

Speake, B. and Whelan, E. (1977) *Young Persons' Work Preparation Courses: A Systematic Evaluation.* (London: Manpower Services Commission).

Speake, B. and Whelan, E. (1985) Developing coping skills in mentally handicapped adults using structured teaching packages. *British Journal of Mental Subnormality,* 62(1), 49–55.

Speake, B. Rhee, K., Basi, L., Shaw, D. and Behan, S. (1991) Identifying individuals with learning disabilities whose behaviour challenges our services. *Research Policy and Planning,* 9, 2, 17–30.

Walsh, P., Coyle, K. and Lynch, C. (1988) The Partners Project: community based recreation for adults with mental handicaps. *Mental Handicap,* 16, 122–125.

Whelan, E. and Reiter, S. (1980) *The Illustrated Vocational Inventory* (Manchester: Copewell Publications).

Zisfein, L. and Rosen, M. (1984) Effects of a personal adjustment training group counselling program. *Mental Retardation,* 12, 50–53.

References to Chapter Ten

Batty, L. (1966) The Chatterly Syndrome. In Hunt, P. (Ed.) *Stigma: The Experience of Disability* (London: Geoffrey Chapman).

Bayliss, P.F.C. (1987) *An Introduction to the Law relating to the Health Care Professions* (Beckenham: Ravenswood Publications).

Brown, R.I. (1988) *Quality of Life for Handicapped People* (London: Croom Helm).

Craft, A. (1991) *Living Your Life: A sex education and personal development programme for students with severe learning difficulties* (Wisbech: LDA Publications).

Department of Health (1991) *Social Care for Adults with Learning Disabilities (Mental Handicap)* (London: Department of Health).

Gold, M. (1976) *A New Definition of Mental Retardation.* Unpublished paper, University of Illinois, USA.

Mahatma Gandhi (1948) Non-violence in Peace and War. Taken from *International Thesaurus of Quotations, 1970* (Harmondsworth: Penguin).

Harris Poll (1991) *Public Attitudes Toward People with Disabilities* (Washington: National Organisation on Disability).

Humphreys, S., Blunden, R., Wilson, C., Newman, T. and Pagler, P. (1985) *Planning for Progress: A colloborative evaluation of the Individual Planning System in NIMROD, Research report 18* (Cardiff: Mental Handicap in Wales, Applied Research Unit).

Larson, S.A. and Lakin, K.C. (1992) Direct-Care Staff Stability in a National Sample of Small Group Homes. *Mental Retardation, 30,* 13–22.

Lundstrom-Roche, F. (1981) *Our Lives* (Dublin: National Committee for the International Year of Disabled People).

McConkey, R. (1992) *Fact Sheets on Mental Handicap* (Melrose: Educating Communities Network).

McConkey, R. and Murphy, R. (1989) A national survey of centres and workshops for adult persons with mental handicap. In McConkey, R. and Conliffe, C. (Eds.) *The Person with Mental Handicap: Preparation for an adult life in the community* (Dublin: St. Michael's House).

Richardson, A. and Ritchie, J. (1986) *Making the Break: Parents' views about adults with a mental handicap leaving home* (London: King's Fund Centre).

Ryan, J. (1980)*The Politics of Mental Handicap* (Harmondsworth: Penguin).

Seed, P. (1988) *Day Care at the Crossroads* (Tunbridge Wells: Costello).

Sutcliffe, J. (1990) *Adults with Learning Difficulties: Education for Choice and Empowerment* (Leicester National Institute of Adult and Continuing Education and Open University Press).

Towell, D. (1988) *An Ordinary Life in Practice: Developing comprehensive community-based services for people with learning difficulties* (London: King's Fund Centre).

Walsh, P. (1988) Handicapped and Female: Two disabilities? In McConkey, R. and McGinley, P. (Eds.) *Concepts and Controversies in Services for People with Mental Handicap* (Galway: Brothers of Charity).

Index

174